WE ARE A PEOPLE!

WE ARE A PEOPLE!

Initiatives in Hispanic American Theology

Edited by
Roberto S. Goizueta

FORTRESS PRESS   Minneapolis

A mi familia

WE ARE A PEOPLE!

Initiatives in Hispanic American Theology

Cover design: Jim Gerhard

Cover art: "La esperanza"/"A celebration of hope," by the Youth Committee of Salvadoran refugees, Colomoncagua, Honduras. Courtesy of Voices on the Border and Refugee Voices.

Library of Congress Cataloging-in-Publication Data

We are a people! : initiatives in Hispanic American theology / edited
   by Roberto S. Goizueta.
         p.   cm.
   Includes bibliographical references.
   ISBN 0-8006-2577-3 : $
   1. Hispanic Americans—Religion.   2. Theology, Doctrinal—
History—20th century.   I. Goizueta, Roberto S.
BR1113.J4W4   1992
230'.089'68073—dc20   92-23666
                                                                 CIP

The paper used in this publication meets the minimum requirements of American National Standard for Information Sciences—Permanence of Paper for Printed Library Materials, ANSI Z329.48-1984.   ∞ ™

Manufactured in the U.S.A.   AF 1-2577
95   94   93   92   1   2   3   4   5   6   7   8   9   10

Contents

Preface

"Hispanic," "Latino," "Hispanic American," or "U.S. Hispanic"—we are all these, and more. The theological work in this volume reflects a process of struggle, the struggle to articulate the complex but profound meaning of a people's historical experience and the significance of that experience for a society itself grappling with the question, "What does it mean to be an American?" Like that of the larger society, the history of Latinos is fraught with contradictions. A people exiled in a foreign land, we nevertheless called this vast land home long before it was "settled" by the Pilgrims. We are a people whose richly hued countenances and accented language bear witness to a history of conflict, out of which, like the mythical phoenix, emerged a new reality, that of the U.S. Hispanic. Born in this clash of cultures, our very identity is seemingly contradictory. Exiles in our own land, we speak the languages, pray to the gods, and sway to the rhythms of the Native American and the Spaniard, the African and the Anglo. Never one or the other but always both at the same time, we are strangers to all.

Although we are children of contradiction, we are also pro-
genitors of reconciliation. The lifeblood that courses through
our veins testifies to the possibility—indeed the necessity—of
human reconciliation. To be a Hispanic living in the United
States is to be a child of conflict and, at the same time, a prophet
of reconciliation. In a world where national borders are becoming increasingly fluid and porous, where communication can
be virtually instantaneous, where "globalization" is no longer
perceived as merely an option but as a necessity for the survival
of any economic or political enterprise, the U.S. Hispanic stands
as a living reminder that, in the face of the ever-present conflicts,
human reconciliation is not an illusory ideal but an attainable
goal, not a threat to be feared but a promise to be fulfilled.
Mestizos and mulattos,[1] heirs to the spiritual wealth of so many
cultures, Latinos are the harbingers of a new American reality,
where other cultures and peoples will no longer be perceived
as threatening "American identity," but will be welcomed as
enriching that identity. If the first five hundred years of *mestizaje*
(the experience of racial and cultural mixture) were constructed
on the backs of millions of victims, our forefathers and fore-
mothers, the next five hundred years will be constructed on the
unquenchable hope that those victims embodied, a hope now
bequeathed to their children.

The Hispanic presence in the United States can no longer be
ignored. The warrants of such an assertion are many: demographic, political, economic, and pastoral. Yet underlying all of
them is a still more basic reason: the U.S. Hispanic community
is a microcosm, paradigm, or symbol of the global community

---

1. Mestizo and mulatto refer to people of mixed race and/or cultural
heritage. Traditionally, the first has referred to people of mixed European and
Native American (Amerindian) heritage, whereas the latter has referred to
people of mixed European and African heritage. In the U.S. Hispanic context,
however, mestizo is sometimes used generically (especially in its noun form
mestizaje) to signify either of the above.

of the twenty-first century. The future of the Americas and, indeed, of the globe, will depend on our ability to confront effectively the global reality of *mestizaje* and to allow that reality to enrich our self-understanding, our understanding of what it means to be an American, of what it means to be human, and consequently of the God who has chosen to be revealed in that humanity.

Recognizing the need to reflect on and articulate the theological significance of the Latino reality, and to do so in dialogue with the larger society that is itself a part of that reality (after all, we are *U.S.* Hispanics), Latino theologians are becoming increasingly prolific. This fact is reflected not only in their growing list of publications but also in the formation and success of such professional associations as La Comunidad of Hispanic American Scholars of Theology and Religion, and the Academy of Catholic Hispanic Theologians of the United States (ACHTUS). Members of these organizations promote the development of theological reflection from the perspective of U.S. Hispanics; that is, out of a self-conscious commitment to the historical experience of Hispanic communities specifically in the United States, which is rooted in but is also distinct from the experience of communities in Latin America. In so doing, U.S. Hispanic theologians promote what has come to be known as a *teología de conjunto* or collaborative theology.

It was out of a desire to encourage such theological reflection that a national conference was convened in June 1990 at Emory University in Atlanta. Sponsored by ACHTUS and the Aquinas Center of Theology, a center for Roman Catholic studies at Emory University, the conference brought together two hundred participants to address these crucial issues. The participants came from every walk of life and every area of the country. Most were Catholic, but a number represented evangelical and mainline Protestant churches. The title of the conference, *¡Somos un Pueblo!* (We Are A People), itself reflected the complexity of our reality. Although we are indeed one people, we are also what Orlando Espín has called a "community of communities," a varied and diverse people.

The idea for this volume of essays by members of ACHTUS was born in that conference. Three of the essays (Deck, Aquino, Espín) were originally presented at the Atlanta conference. With the encouragement of Michael West, senior editor at Fortress Press, the project began to take shape. I am therefore deeply indebted to him and to Fortress Press for their farsighted commitment to this relatively new theological movement and for their invaluable editorial assistance in the preparation of this volume. I am also grateful to President James T. Laney of Emory University and Dean Jim L. Waits of Emory's Candler School of Theology for their support.

One of the most difficult issues that surfaced in the editorial process was the question of language. As indicated above, that question cuts to the very heart of our identity as U.S. Hispanics. As U.S. Hispanic theologians, we have often been raised in Spanish-speaking households but have received our professional training in English. Consequently, the task of communicating our experience to the larger society often involves, literally, a process of translation. This hard reality, always a painful one for us to confront, symbolizes the entire experience of U.S. Hispanics. While every day we grapple with the question of what it means to be both Hispanic and North American, the society continually forces us to choose one or the other, as if these were mutually exclusive. Often—maybe too often—pragmatic considerations become determinative.

That is the case in this volume. Ideally, of course, each essay would appear in both Spanish and English. Given the inevitable financial and time constraints, the only practical possibility was their publication in English; as the essays are primarily geared toward a North American college-educated audience, most of the readership will be either bilingual or English monolingual.

This choice was not made, however, without deep regret and a considerable amount of uneasiness. The Spanish language remains an important symbol for Latinos. We hope that publication of books like this will help bring about a society in which U.S. Hispanics no longer have to choose between their identity as Hispanics and their identity as North Americans.

A similar and equally complex issue faced in the editorial process was terminological: deciding whether to use the term *Hispanic, Hispanic American, U.S. Hispanic, Latino, Latin, or Latin American.* Again, this problem merely reflects the complex historical situation of Hispanics living in the United States. (In the first part of his essay, Fernando Segovia discusses that complexity and the consequent difficulty of arriving at a satisfactory solution to the terminological problem.) None of the above terms is fully adequate, and all had their origins outside the Latino community itself. While I prefer the term *U.S. Hispanic* because of its specificity, I sometimes use other terms interchangeably, out of a desire to reflect, in my vocabulary, the complexity of our historical reality. In discussing the chapters in this volume, however, I have attempted in each case to use the term(s) used by the particular author.

The historical ramifications of the cultural and linguistic situation described above are addressed in the volume's first essay, by Allan Figueroa Deck. Deck underscores the diversity that exists within the Latino community itself. He views this complex reality through the lens of a U.S. Hispanic Catholicism whose history and worldview are often at odds with the Anglo American Catholicism dominant in our society. He argues for a greater pastoral outreach to Hispanics as well as greater support for the development of Hispanic intellectual leaders.

Citing a prevailing tendency to romanticize the history of immigrant groups in the United States, Deck reminds us that every process of assimilation was accompanied by much struggle and conflict. He suggests that the historical experience of U.S. Hispanics can generate important insights into the history of the United States and the history of Catholicism. That experience has been tragically ignored in most debates among Anglo Catholics (debates about "American" Catholicism) or between Anglo American Catholics and Rome. One example of how the U.S. Hispanic experience can provide new historical insight is reflected in Deck's desire to revisit such historically popular— and presently unpopular—models as the national parish, which would promote grass-roots cultural identity before encouraging hasty integration into artificially created "multicultural" communities that stifle Hispanic identity.

Finally, Deck warns that, as the Anglo American churches become increasingly middle-class, the danger of cultural assimilation is accompanied by that of class assimilation and the concomitant alienation of poor Hispanics from upwardly mobile, middle-class Hispanics. Deck's essay ends with a plea for the development of scholars and intellectuals, especially theologians, rooted in U.S. Hispanic communities and able to help those communities avert these dangers and address their most pressing problems.

As Deck explains the significance of our social location for reading history and bringing that history to bear on present issues, so Fernando Segovia analyzes the significance of our social location for reading the central historical texts of the Christian community, the Scriptures. After discussing the profound and broad-ranging impact that recent recognition of the importance of social location has had on all the scholarly disciplines and on the intellectual enterprise as such, Segovia pinpoints the significance of the Hispanic American social location for that enterprise. In the face of the internal diversity and complexity of the Hispanic American community, he warns against oversimplifying the Hispanic American social location, as if it were a uniform, monolithic reality. At the same time, he notes the increasing tendency of the various Hispanic American subgroups—for example, Cuban Americans and Mexican Americans—to identify themselves as Hispanic Americans, thereby stressing their similarities rather than their differences. This process of consolidation is also evident in the work of Hispanic American theologians and exegetes, who have sought to read the Scriptures and the Christian faith through Hispanic American lenses. To illustrate the process by which the Hispanic American experience influences the reading of Scripture, Segovia analyzes the work of four Hispanic American theologians, each of whom comes from a different personal background: (1) Ada María Isasi-Díaz, a Cuban American, Roman Catholic laywoman; (2) Harold J. Recinos, a Puerto Rican, United Methodist minister born in New York City; (3) Virgilio Elizondo, the Mexican American rector of San Fernando Cathedral in San Antonio, Texas, and founder of the Mexican American Cultural Center; and (4) Justo L. González, a Cuban American, United Methodist minister.

According to Segovia, the work of each of these important figures reflects the influence of liberation theology as a methodology, as a perspective from which to read Scripture. At the same time, each writer's particular social location also provides distinctive insights into the meaning of the biblical texts. Isasi-Díaz's writing reflects a U.S. Hispanic women's or *mujerista* theological perspective, which calls into question sexist and racist (mis)appropriations of the texts. Recinos articulates the significance of the barrio (neighborhood) as a social location, or perspective from which to read Scripture, which reading can then engender a liberating pastoral theology for the barrio. Elizondo's self-conscious and explicit social location is that of *mestizaje*. That experience yields rich insights into Jesus' own social location as a Galilean, a mestizo from the borderlands, and hence into the meaning of his message. Finally, Segovia cites González's book *Mañana* as providing the most systematic and explicit articulation of a Hispanic American biblical her-meneutics. For González, a central characteristic of the Hispanic American social location, within which the biblical texts are read, is the shared experience of exile that unites all Hispanic Americans and gives birth to liberation. In his conclusion, Se-govia discusses the liberating methodology that unites all four theologians, while examining how each theologian's own social location influences his or her interpretation of liberation and the liberating message of Scripture.

While Segovia focuses on the import of the Hispanic Amer-ican social location for the reading of Scripture, I explore, in my chapter, the import of the U.S. Hispanic experience for theological method itself and hence for the theologian's under-standing of her or his task. As that understanding will be greatly influenced by how the theologian implicitly or explicitly per-ceives the relationship between theory and praxis, I focus my discussion on the ways in which U.S. Hispanic experience can deepen our understanding of that relationship. In dialogue with key Western philosophers and theologians who have addressed this issue, I suggest that, in the light of our historical experience and our worldview, U.S. Hispanics can counter many of the oppressive distortions of modern Western thought. We can do this by emphasizing the inherently aesthetic and communal char-acter of human activity so evident in our *manera de ser*, or way of life. At the same time, I warn against romanticizing and thus distorting U.S. Hispanic praxis by interpreting it as anti-intellectual and based in feelings. Such an idealization would simply reinforce the dominant culture's oppressive stereotypes of U.S. Hispanics.

I contend that, to avoid idealizing aesthetics and affect in U.S. Hispanic praxis, we must take seriously—in a foundational and systematic way—the experience of U.S. Hispanic women. The implications of doing so are developed further in the fol-lowing chapter, by María Pilar Aquino. That she identifies her perspective as Latin American is indicative of the diversity of the U.S. Hispanic community: for several years a professor at Mount St. Mary's College in Los Angeles, the Mexican-born Aquino continues to identify strongly with her Latin American roots (more so, perhaps, than U.S. Hispanics who may have emigrated as young children or were born in the United States) while nevertheless struggling, like all of us, to define what it means to be a Latin American living in the United States.

Sympathetic to Latin American liberation theology and Anglo American feminism, Aquino nevertheless proffers a critique of both: the first for its male-centered perspective, and the latter for its failure to make explicit the causal link between sexism and classism, between the privileges of First World women and the exploitation of Third World women. Such a critique is essential as Latinas develop a theological reflection which affirms them as historical subjects in their own right. In turn, this reflection contributes to the development of an integral theological perspective which will be liberating for both women and men.

Aquino examines the key methodological characteristics of a liberation theology done from the perspective of Latin American women to demonstrate how such a theology can contribute to the development of an integral theological perspective. Some of these characteristics are shared with traditional Christian theologies; it will, for example, insist on the ecclesial dimension of theology. Other characteristics distinguish the theological reflection of Latina women from traditional theologies; for example, liberation theology done by women is praxis-based, as opposed to traditional theologies, which have tended to be word-centered. Yet this praxis-based reflection does not reject reason; rather it dialectically relates life and thought, feeling and intellect.

Sixto García also emphasizes the integral and integrating task of theology. He demonstrates how the holistic worldview of Hispanics can contribute to the theological enterprise in general and trinitarian theology in particular. Pointing to popular religiosity as an important source for Hispanic theology, he discovers, within popular religiosity, a holistic "popular hermeneutic" that relates celebration, reflection, belief, and praxis. If a Hispanic theologian grounds her or his reflection in the life of Hispanic communities, then the theologian's role will include not only that of the thinker but also those of the poet and the prophet.

García examines the significance of such a methodology, and of a Hispanic perspective, for our understanding of the Trinity. Again looking to popular religiosity, especially passion plays, García underscores the christocentric character of the Hispanic understanding of God. In devotion to Mary, another important aspect of popular religiosity, García discovers a pneumatological significance: "Mary becomes the sign of the Spirit of holiness and healing for suffering and marginalized Hispanic faith communities." Despite the inevitable pietistic exaggerations, Marian devotions reveal Mary as a sign of hope and liberation for Hispanic communities. As García further develops the liberating dimensions of a Hispanic view of the Trinity, he presents a critique of "theologically and socially dysfunctional" Western views of the Trinity.

The liberating, hope-filled view of God characteristic of Hispanic popular religiosity also has important implications for our understanding of grace—that is, how God is present in the world—and the role of culture as a mediator of grace. These implications are explored in the final chapter, by Orlando Espín. If the incarnate God of Christians is revealed in and through our humanness, that humanness is itself expressed in and through culture. All cultures are (imperfect) mediators of God's presence. Consequently, any attempt to denude the faith of U.S. Hispanics of its specifically Hispanic character not only dehumanizes Hispanics but also obstructs God's self-revelation. Insofar as popular religiosity is a privileged "locus of Hispanic self-disclosure," reflecting the values most important to Hispanics (for example, family and community), it is also a privileged locus of God's liberating self-revelation to our communities.

The order of the theological forays presented in this volume is itself meant to illustrate, for the reader, the methodology either explicitly endorsed or implicitly present in all of them, a methodology that grounds the interpretation of Christian doctrine in the historical experience of the faith community. Deck introduces the reader to the historical experience of U.S. Hispanics. Then Segovia, myself, and Aquino focus explicitly on the question, "How does that experience influence the way we, as Christians, do theology?" Finally, García and Espín ask, "How does the way we do theology influence our understanding of traditional Christian doctrines?"

It is my sincere hope that this volume will be a source of inspiration for U.S. Hispanics struggling to find acceptance as Christians and Americans without having to deny their Hispanic identity, and a source of edification for Anglos seeking to understand the U.S. Hispanic reality. Although primarily addressed to a theological or seminary audience, the essays ought to be of interest to nontheologians as well; one cannot understand U.S. Hispanic culture unless one understands the deepseated, religious, and spiritual sensibilities permeating the culture. This, indeed, may be the central message of our book.

Roberto S. Goizueta

Contributors

María Pilar Aquino
Director of the Hispanic Ministry Program at Mount St. Mary's College (Los Angeles). This involves teaching theology and training women and men to work among the Spanish-speaking popular sectors. A Mexican theologian, she received her STB and STL in Mexico and Brazil and earned her doctoral degree at the Universidad Pontificia de Salamanca, Spain. She is the author of the first book ever published on Latin American feminist theology, *Nuestro clamor por la vida: Teología Latinoamericana desde la perspectiva de la mujer* (DEI, 1992). She is also the editor of the book *Aportes para una teología desde la mujer* (Biblia y Fe, 1988), and she has written several articles addressing this perspective. A member of the Ecumenical Association of Third World Theologians, she is also one of the founders of the Academy of Catholic Hispanic Theologians of the United States.

Allan Figueroa Deck, S.J.
Coordinator of Hispanic pastoral studies in the Pastoral Studies Center of Loyola Marymount University, Los Angeles. Earned a doctorate in Latin American studies at St. Louis University and another in Missiology at the Gregorian University. Previously he was assistant

professor of Hispanic studies and missiology at the Jesuit School of Theology at Berkeley, California. In addition to academic work, Father Deck has been actively involved in pastoral and social justice ministries. He was pastor of Guadalupe Church in Santa Ana, California, from 1976 to 1979 and director of Hispanic ministry for the Diocese of Orange (California) from 1979 to 1985. He has served as president of the Jesuit Hispanic Ministry Conference and was the cofounder and first president of the Academy of Catholic Hispanic Theologians of the United States. He is currently president of the National Catholic Council for Hispanic Ministry and consultant to the U.S. Bishops' Committee on Hispanic Affairs. His book *The Second Wave: Hispanic Ministry and the Evangelization of Cultures* (Paulist Press, 1989) received first place in the professional category of the 1989 award ceremony of the Catholic Press Association. His most recent book, *Frontiers of Hispanic Theology in the United States*, of which he is editor, is published by Orbis Books.

Orlando O. Espín
Associate Professor of Theology at the University of San Diego. He earned a doctorate in systematics at the Catholic University of Rio de Janeiro (Brazil), and has since taught in both Latin America and the United States. He is the current president of the Academy of Catholic Hispanic Theologians of the United States. His research and publications have concentrated on the study of Latino popular religion.

Sixto J. García
Professor of Theology at St. Vincent de Paul Regional Seminary, Boynton Beach, Florida. He received his Ph.D. in theology from the University of Notre Dame in 1986. With Orlando Espín, he has presented seminars on Hispanic American theology at the annual Catholic Theological Society of America convention. Since 1986 he has taught candidates for the Permanent Diaconate in the Permanent Diaconate Program of the Archdiocese of Miami and has been engaged in parish biblical and theological study groups at the parishes of St. Agnes, St. Agatha, and St. Dominic, of the Archdiocese of Miami, and at St. Ignatius Cathedral, Diocese of Palm Beach.

Roberto S. Goizueta
Associate Professor of Theology at Loyola University of Chicago. He received his doctorate from Marquette University. He is past president of the Academy of Catholic Hispanic Theologians of the United States, served as co-director of the Aquinas Center of Theology at Emory University, Atlanta, and taught at Loyola University, New Orleans. Goizueta is the author of *Liberation, Method, and Dialogue* (1988).

Fernando F. Segovia
Professor of New Testament and Early Christian Literature at Vanderbilt Divinity School, Nashville, Tennessee. He earned his doctoral degree from the University of Notre Dame. Presently, he is at work on three fronts involving the development of a theology of otherness and mixture, a hermeneutics of otherness and engagement, and a literary methodology of intercultural criticism. The author of *The Farewell of the Word: The Johannine Call to Abide* (Fortress Press, 1991), he is currently engaged in several forthcoming projects for Fortress Press.

1

At the Crossroads:
North American and Hispanic

Allan Figueroa Deck, S.J.

One of the most prolific and influential theologians of our time, the French Dominican Yves Congar, once wrote: "It is not unreasonable to suppose that one day our pagan continent (Europe) might be re-evangelized by coloured people, the pagans of yesterday, the Christians of today and tomorrow."[1] Congar was among the first to acknowledge the need for a new attitude toward the peoples of color and other marginated Third World peoples on the part of Europeans and North Americans. No longer will paternalistic or condescending attitudes do. A reversal of roles is taking place by which the oppressed and marginal enter into their own and assume their day in the sun.

Now is an important moment in the articulation of that new attitude, especially as it relates to the numerous and diverse Hispanic communities in the United States. These communities, along with their African American and Asian-Pacific contemporaries, are at the vanguard in that process of gestation that is giving birth to the United States of the next century.

---

1. Yves Congar, *Christians Active in the World* (New York: Herder and Herder, 1968), 200.

In a recent publication entitled *The Second Wave*, I discuss
the basis for the changing attitude toward U.S. Hispanics within
the Roman Catholic context. The basis has to do with the magnitude of the demographic changes taking place in today's American society and Catholic church.[2] The title was an effort to
highlight the present moment of change as an especially critical
one. My study was focused on the implications of this sea of
change for the daily conduct, planning, commitments, and tone
of U.S. Catholicism. Fully one-third of today's U.S. Catholics
are Hispanic. Conservatively we can project that Hispanics will
constitute half of the Catholic population early in the next century.[3] Here I would like to highlight some fundamental issues
that need to be addressed in light of this change. In so doing,
I hope to provide a framework for thinking theologically about
U.S. Hispanic history, culture, and tradition.

The Inadequacy of the Immigrant Analogy

Roman Catholics have become so accustomed to think of
ourselves in terms of the historic immigrant pattern of decades
past that we resist rethinking our current reality in the more
subtle terms appropriate for the Hispanic experience. The immigrant analogy is not adequate for grasping the Hispanic experience, because Hispanic roots in what is now the United
States are more ancient than the Anglo American ones. To the
extent that the immigrant analogy is appropriate it must be
nuanced by such significant facts as the symbiotic relationship
of Hispanic immigrants, at least the largest groups of them—

2. Allan Figueroa Deck, S.J., *The Second Wave: Hispanic Ministry and the
Evangelization of Cultures* (Mahwah, N.J.: Paulist Press, 1989).
3. For a recent demographic report, see Ruth T. Doyle, "Ethnic Populations in the U.S." (New York: Office of Pastoral Research, Archdiocese of
New York, 1988).

the Mexicans and the Puerto Ricans—with their homeland.[4] It is also relevant to note that the Spanish language, unlike the languages of other immigrant groups, is not "foreign." Spanish is the second language of the United States and has been continuously spoken in the American Southwest from the sixteenth century onwards.[5]

Hispanics: Strangers in Their Own Land and Church

The marginality of Hispanics within North American society and the church is a complex matter that needs to be understood at the outset. Certainly one of the factors is the strong anti-Hispanic bias of Anglo American culture. That bias has been traced back over centuries to the imperial rivalry between Spain and England and to the worldwide propaganda against Spain and things Spanish called the Black Legend.[6] Linked to this, of course, were the bitter polemics of the Reformation and the Counter-Reformation. Spain herself became marginalized from the modern world through her strident identification with Catholicism, especially the distinctive Spanish brand forged in the Reconquest. Hispanic Catholicism, moreover, rooted itself to the indigenous cultures of the Americas in the sixteenth century, a century before Anglo American Protestants or Catholics set foot on North American soil. Already in the sixteenth century Spain and Portugal were importing slaves from Africa. Another

---

4. The dramatic changes taking place in the socialist world may mean that even Castro's Cuba may soon open up to the return or visits of Cuban Americans to their homeland. Thus this important Hispanic group will begin an international symbiosis similar to that of Mexican Americans and Puerto Ricans.

5. Alfredo Mirandé discusses the immigrant analogy and other historical and social science paradigms in *The Chicano Experience: An Alternative Perspective* (Notre Dame, Ind.: University of Notre Dame Press, 1985), 185–200.

6. See Philip Wayne Powell, *Tree of Hate: Propaganda and Prejudices Affecting United States Relations with the Hispanic World* (New York: Basic Books, 1971).

important branch of Hispanic American culture was born in the Antilles and the coast of Central and South America as the Spaniards and Africans forged a new mulatto race. Such an intense miscegenation never occurred in the Anglo American colonies, where colonization involved the transfer of preexisting European patterns upon a wilderness. In Hispanic America, by contrast, a complex hybrid was being forged. Hence the starting points for these two cultures—the Hispanic American and the Anglo American—are drastically different.[7]

Anglo American Catholicism is rooted in the experience of the eighteenth-century English Catholic settlers of Maryland. These people were truly English. They were also Catholic, yet imbued with the culture of modernity that Great Britain disseminated through its legal system, burgeoning commerce and industry, and its relatively democratic ideology. American Catholics of the eighteenth century were loyal British subjects, members of the unique culture being forged in the North American colonies and soon in the new American nation. They had been exposed to a vibrant capitalism and were themselves largely bourgeois and quite literate.[8] Even when huge waves of working-class or peasant-class immigrants began to swell the ranks of the U.S. Catholic church, its Anglo American character remained.[9]

7. See Virgilio Elizondo, *The Galilean Journey: The Mexican American Promise* (Maryknoll, N.Y.: Orbis Books, 1983) and *The Future Is Mestizo: Life Where Cultures Meet* (Bloomington, Ind.: Meyer-Stone Books, 1988).

8. Joseph P. Chinnici, speaking of the early Anglo American Catholics, states: ". . . to a degree greater than has been realized, American Catholics participated in the mentality of the Enlightenment." See Chinnici, "American Catholics and Religious Pluralism, 1775–1820," *Journal of Ecumenical Studies* 16 (Fall 1977): 736.

9. Jay Dolan describes the American Catholicism championed by prominent bishops such as John Ireland, John Keane, and others in the last decade of the nineteenth century in *The American Catholic Experience* (New York: Doubleday & Co., 1985), 294–320.

Virgilio Elizondo has characterized this Catholicism as "Nordic." That is, it has a certain affinity to the Catholicism of Northern Europe, whence the vast majority of Catholic immigrants came.[10] These Catholics struggled throughout the nineteenth century to achieve recognition and status in an overwhelmingly Protestant land. In several important ways these Catholics *did* become American. They assimilated. In addition to the many positive cultural values acquired through Americanization, there may have been some disvalues for instance, a certain strain of Anglo American racism directed against blacks, Native Americans, half-breeds, Hispanics, Asians, and any other non-Anglo racial type.[11]

The intellectual culture of North American Catholics was profoundly influenced by this American experience, imbuing U.S. Catholic leaders with concerns, interests, and perhaps even biases that would render the comprehension of things Hispanic problematic. Certainly one of those qualities was a predilection for more articulate, rational exposition of faith. Church historian Patrick Carey has contended that the importance placed on reason is a characteristic mark of United States Catholicism, but in the case of Hispanic Catholicism the opposite is true.[12] What was stressed by the original Spanish missioners was the grafting of Catholic faith onto the rich vine of indigenous ritual, symbol, and myth. In their work with Native Americans, as it were, the Spanish missioners stressed feeling compunction more than

10. Virgilio Elizondo, *Christianity and Culture* (San Antonio: Mexican American Cultural Center, 1975), 156–57.

11. Reginald Horsman, *Race and Manifest Destiny: The Origins of American Racial Anglo-Saxonism* (Cambridge: Harvard University Press, 1981), esp. chap. 11, "Anglo-Saxons and Mexicans," 208–28.

12. Lecture by Patrick Carey delivered at John Carroll University on October 26, 1989. For the Hispanic case, see Moisés Sandoval, ed., *Fronteras: A History of Latin American Church in the USA Since 1513* (San Antonio: Mexican American Cultural Center, 1983), esp. pt. 2, "The Church in Conflict (1809–1898)," 141–221.

defining it. As might be expected, then, the encounter between Anglo American and European Catholics with Hispanic Catholics in the Southwest in the second half of the nineteenth century was rather conflictual. It has tended to remain so to this day. Their cultures and religious orientations were quite distinct; consequently, Hispanics from the very beginning of their involvement with the United States have been outsiders. They have tended to remain outsiders in both church and society.

Hispanics' perspectives on U.S. church history (like the one just suggested) have yet to find full expression. U.S. Catholic intellectuals have been almost totally dependent upon the European-based and indigenous, Anglo American intellectual culture.[13] The Hispanic American world remains peripheral at best.

The Hispanic American world, however, has begun to impinge on Anglo American intellectual life, especially on its Catholic element. This is the result of trends advanced by the Second Vatican Council: the awakening of sociopolitical, economic, and theological reflection in Latin America; and the rise of "the world church," as Karl Rahner called it. One interesting by-product of this development is the emergence of the Spanish language as a serious tool for theological reflection. It is now accepted, for instance, by a growing number of graduate schools as satisfying the doctoral language requirement. By and large, though, the strong undergirding of U.S. Catholicism in Anglo American culture means that there will continue to be conflict between that Catholicism and its Hispanic counterpart as demographic changes inexorably challenge the strong Anglo American foundations of U.S. Catholicism.

While the U.S. Catholic bishops have expressed a sincere commitment to affirming the Hispanic presence as a blessing,

13. John A. Coleman makes this point strenuously in *An American Strategic Theology* (New York: Paulist Press, 1982), esp. 157. See also Jay Dolan, *The Immigrant Church* (Baltimore: Johns Hopkins University Press, 1975).

the cultural and intellectual bases for translating that commitment into ongoing dialogue, mutual respect, and deeper understanding are lacking.[14] That lack of insight into the diverse cultural starting points of Anglo American Catholicism (which, ironically, is very Irish) and Latin American Catholicism is due, perhaps more than anything else, to the lack of intellectual leaders among U.S. Hispanics. If they do not articulate their experiences, who will? Mainline, Anglo American scholars, perhaps understandably, have not displayed a great deal of interest in the Hispanic aspect of the church's life. The dearth of serious studies of the Hispanic presence in church contexts is especially appalling since the church's future has a great deal to do with that issue. This may reflect the lack of interest on the part of graduate schools, Catholic and secular, in Hispanic questions and concerns. Whatever be the explanation for the lack of serious reflection on the Hispanic presence in church and society, the fact remains that the pastoral outreach of the church to U.S. Hispanics will falter if it is not accompanied by in-depth reflection of a historical, socioeconomic, political, cultural, and theological nature. That reflection is lacking.[15]

The often-observed growth of evangelical and fundamentalist Hispanic congregations throughout the United States gives witness, for example, to the inadequacy of current outreach efforts.[16] This phenomenon is due, at least in part, to the lack

14. *The Hispanic Presence: Challenge and Commitment,* U.S. Bishops' Pastoral Letter (Washington, D.C.: United States Catholic Conference 1984).

15. Emblematic of the failure to produce intellectual leaders among U.S. Hispanic Catholics are the following statistics taken from William Baumgaertner, ed., *Fact Book on Theological Education 1987–88* (Vandalia, Ohio: Association of Theological Schools, 1988), 93, 110: A total of 958 Hispanics were enrolled in Protestant theological seminaries and centers, while only 280 were in Catholic seminaries and theological centers. One might infer that tomorrow's (if not today's) Hispanic theological leaders will be Protestant.

16. Allan Figueroa Deck, "Proselytism and Hispanic Catholics: How Long Can We Cry Wolf?" *America,* 10 December 1988, 485–89.

of a critical understanding of the Hispanic people, their Catholicism, and their cultures. Consequently, pastoral praxis has tended to be unadapted, poorly adapted, or mistakenly adapted all with disastrous results in terms of winning or retaining the loyalty of Hispanic Catholics.

I would like to turn, therefore, to some specific historical themes that in my judgment are critical in understanding the reality of Hispanics in today's North American Catholic church. These are some of the themes that await more rigorous reflection as scholars arise who are imbued with Hispanic historical perspectives.

The Nineteenth-Century Experience: The Immigrant Church

Studies of the North American Catholic church, as I have already suggested, tend to reflect a mainstream perspective. The formative period in the evolution of the prevailing mythos was the nineteenth and early twentieth centuries. Today's U.S. Catholic is very aware of the long and seemingly decisive immigrant phase of that history. Generally, that period has been interpreted in such a way as to reinforce the status quo. It is viewed as a definitively transcended phase that has inexorably led up to today's multicultural church. Certain assumptions and omissions are made regarding that previous phase. Some of these assumptions are, from a Hispanic viewpoint, deceptive.

While it is acknowledged that there was a place for all the ethnic groups, the conflictual character of their struggle to thrive in the U.S. church tends to be overlooked. The truth is that the various Catholic ethnic groups came to feel at home only after considerable struggle. Silvano Tomasi documents the long and arduous path of Italians in their struggle to obtain the pastoral care necessary to maintain their loyalty to the church in the United States.[17] It is frequently noted that Hispanics were the first group to come to the United States without their own clergy. This is not exactly true. The Italians came without clergy. Only after "raising holy hell" in Rome and working together with sizable groups of disgruntled German American Catholics did the Italians find acceptance and a modus vivendi in the U.S. church.[18] Significant numbers of priests were sent from Italy and began to staff national parishes. The Propaganda Fide generally looked upon the national parishes with sympathy, while the American hierarchy in general feared what they called the rising nationalism of the various immigrant groups.[19]

The impression conveyed today is that Hispanics will receive their just share of attention and resources from the church through friendly persuasion and by simply articulating the merits of their case. Did not the church historically meet the needs of previous immigrant groups? Yes, but not without a considerable amount of pushing. The clergy were necessarily at the front line of this sometimes bloody battle. The Irish had priests who fought for them, as did the Germans and eventually the Italians. Hispanics, in contrast, have suffered a chronic shortage of priests. Insofar as there have been Hispanic priests to assume this crucial role, they appear to have been relatively less successful than their counterparts of other times in winning recognition and developing services and resources for their people.

To grasp the conflictual character of the role of immigrant and ethnic minority clergy, all one need do is read some of the archival materials reproduced in works such as Tomasi's. The

17. Silvano Tomasi, *Power and Piety* (Staten Island, N.Y.: Center for Migration Studies, 1975).
18. Stephen Michael Di Giovanni documents the situation in New York in the last two decades of the nineteenth century in his doctoral dissertation, "Michael Augustine Corrigan and the Italian Immigrants: The Relationship between the Church and the Italians in the Archdiocese of New York, 1885–1902" (Rome: Gregorian University, 1983).
19. Ibid., 74.

prevailing view is that this was a wonderful period of national churches serenely presided over by Irish American bishops. The truth is much different. There was a high level of controversy and even rancor in the church throughout the closing decades of the nineteenth century and well into the twentieth, caused in large measure by the struggle of new immigrant groups for recognition and territory. The contemporary militancy of Hispanic Catholics has generally been benign by comparison.

Related to the question of the fate of immigrants in the U.S. church is the role of the Holy See, especially the Propaganda Fide, which exercised considerable influence on U.S. church affairs until 1908. Rome was unquestionably a great ally of the immigrant groups. The understanding of Rome's role in that process, however, has frequently been mingled with the famous Americanist controversy. This controversy, along with the papal condemnation of Modernism in 1907 and today's controversies with the Pope and the Roman Curia, is sometimes viewed as part of an undifferentiated, negative Roman influence upon the U.S church. That view, it seems to me, obscures the fact that, at least in the case of the pastoral care of immigrants, Rome has consistently played a positive role, taking the position of the immigrants more to heart than many of our American Catholic church leaders. The address of Archbishop Pio Laghi, former Pro-Nuncio, before the U.S. bishops is only one of innumerable instances of Rome's effort to represent the needs of immigrants before local church authorities.[20] A documentary study of Rome's role with U.S. immigrants, especially Hispanic immigrants, would clarify and, I believe, substantiate my view.[21]

20. Archbishop Pio Laghi, address to the National Conference of Catholic Bishops' General Meeting, 14 November 1988, in *Origins* (Washington, D.C.: USCC Publishing and Promotion), 24 November 1988, 386–89.
21. Both Tomasi's and Di Giovanni's works provide innumerable instances of Rome's concern for immigrants. That concern has been sustained in recent years by the last three popes. See, for instance, Pope Paul VI's *Pastoral Concern*

It is interesting to review today the Americanist controversy of the late nineteenth century in light of the growing literature on inculturation. From today's vantage point it seems that North American progressives like Isaac Hecker and Archbishop Ireland may not have had a sufficient grasp of the difference between certain U.S. cultural values (which they championed) and countercultural gospel values. Perhaps Rome's views of American culture were informed not only by self-interest and restorationism but also by a certain intuitive awareness of the non-evangelical aspects of some of our most touted North American values. Some of the concerns and issues of importance to U.S. Hispanics (such as respect for a more symbolic, intuitive, ritualistic, and corporative faith) may well be better understood in Rome than in the United States. In any case, Rome does provide a counterbalance insofar as it ostensibly reflects the perspectives of worldwide Catholicism upon a special Anglo American brand. Such a balancing role is especially necessary, it seems to me, given the extraordinary power of North American culture on the world scene. That power, linked as it is to the forces of technology, modernization, and secularization, is greater than any power—real or imagined—that Rome may possess.

A Hispanic account of U.S. Catholic church history may serve to demythologize some of our past. Some of the longstanding historical interpretations of past leaders and events may stand to be revised in the process. The Americanist controversy may be one of them.[22] The nature of the U.S. church's relations with Rome may be another.

---

for People on the Move (Washington, D.C.: USCC Publications, 1976). Perhaps something similar could be said with regard to Rome's championing the cause of black Catholics over against the indifference or outright opposition of U.S. church leaders.

22. Gerald P. Fogarty has studied the controversy in depth in *The Vatican and the Americanist Crisis: Denis J. O'Connell, American Agent in Rome, 1885–1903* (Rome: Miscellanea Historiae Pontificia, 1974).

11

The National Parish Revisited

Central to the historical understanding of how Hispanics have fared in the U.S. Catholic church is the question of national parishes. It is interesting to note that Hispanics have not been dealt with pastorally in the way that other ethnic groups in this country have. Hispanics were generally deprived of the instrumentality of national parishes.[23] Roger Finke has documented the fundamental importance of the national parish in maintaining the loyalty of Catholic ethnic groups from 1850 to 1926. He shows how a remarkable support system was fashioned for these newcomers.[24] No such support system has been fashioned for United States Hispanics. Their arrival in large numbers after 1945 occurred after church leadership had generally made up its mind that national parishes were to be tolerated but programmatically eliminated. Undoubtedly there were many reasons for this. My point is simply that massive numbers of Catholic leaders continue to believe that the national parish is some kind of fossil. It is simply not in their purview. Curiously enough, the New Code of Canon Law offers an interesting and flexible alternative called the personal parish. There is hardly a bishop in the United States, however, who has moved ahead with this pastoral remedy.[25]

23. Deck, *The Second Wave*, 59.

24. Roger Finke, "The Coming of the Catholics, 1850–1926," presentation at the 1988 Annual Meeting of the Society for the Scientific Study of Religion in Chicago (unpublished). In addition to the national parish, Finke stresses the importance of (1) having clergy and religious men and women who literally came from the same ethnic groups and social class as the immigrants, and (2) having religious congregations such as the Redemptorists, Passionists, and Jesuits, who provided parish missions that recognized the power of popular devotions and emotions and the need for catharsis among people whose lives had been terribly disoriented by migration.

25. William A. Logar summarizes various points of view regarding the national parish and emphasizes some interesting canonical issues in "I Was a Stranger and You Welcomed Me," in *Today's Immigrants and Refugees* (Washington, D.C.: Office of Pastoral Care of Migrants and Refugees, USCC, 1988), 131–45.

The lack of juridically sanctioned Hispanic parishes with strong pastors identified with their people is perhaps the single greatest reason for the ineffectiveness of our outreach to Hispanics. People will integrate and ultimately unite only from a position of strength. Their stories will be forcefully told only by those who have the voice and the credibility to speak on their behalf. In the Catholic church we know that person is the priest, especially the pastor. With all the good intentions in the world we have tended to move toward integrating Hispanics into our Anglo or mixed parishes. In many instances the results have been discouraging. Hispanics are unwittingly giving the impression that this integrated parish is not for them.[26]

Something else that needs to be analyzed is the long-range effectiveness of the national organizations set up by the Catholic bishops initially through the insistence of Archbishop Robert Lucey starting in the late 1960s. I am referring specifically to the Secretariat for Hispanic Affairs of the United States Catholic Conference and various regional offices of Hispanic affairs. They have done excellent work and have promoted valuable projects on behalf of Hispanics throughout the nation. Most notable among them are the three *encuentro* processes and the National Pastoral Plan for Hispanic Ministry.

My critique of these structures, however, is that they are inadequate and have been rendered somewhat ineffective by the lack of durable, basic institutions like parishes that might translate and communicate the processes coming down from above into viable and practical programs. The basic ecclesial communities, where they do exist, do not possess the authority needed to keep the input below, from the grass-roots level, continuous and strong. While serious efforts continue to be made

26. Jaime Vidal refers to "the fallacy of the integrated parish" in his trenchant account of the status of Hispanic ministry in the eastern United States in *Presencia Nueva* (Newark, N.J.: Archdiocese of Newark, Office of Research and Planning, 1988), 235–351.

to get to the grass-roots levels, the relatively few diocesan and parish structures attuned to the Hispanic reality have made the national and regional offices unable to effect a great deal of change. There is a tendency in the U.S. church to deal with the Hispanic reality in a bureaucratic fashion, that is, creating offices and programs one or several steps removed from the people. That is because sometimes the parishes are hermetically sealed and unresponsive. Not enough key clergy are really interested. This state of affairs relates directly to the lack of viable national or personal parishes, the lack of juridically based and hence, durable and influential structures devoted to the pastoral care of Hispanics. The impersonalism and cold, organizational, and even managerial character of today's so-called pastoral remedies contrast with the spontaneity and personalism of Hispanic cultures. We speak of inculturation of the *pastoral* context while buying the Anglo American *organizational* context and its frequently lock step models at the parish, diocesan, regional, and national levels of church administration. Must not inculturation occur as well at these levels organizationally, or are these aspects of the church's life nonnegotiable?

A practical sense of subsidiarity, moreover, has sometimes been lacking in Hispanic ministry. As a result, a firm ecclesial base in the grass roots has not been created. National and regional offices are important, but they cannot substitute for direct, institutionalized contact with the local communities. The emphasis on the creation of small, faith-sharing, basic ecclesial communities is a positive development. But these communities cannot substitute for parishes, which in the U.S. context especially provide the basis for long-range pastoral effectiveness.

Hispanics and "The American Catholic Moment"

A fuller understanding of the American Catholic church's current status and future has been obscured to some extent by the debate about "the Catholic moment" sparked by Richard

John Neuhaus. This debate has tended to leave Hispanics and the church's demographic transformation out of the picture. Consequently it deforms the reality.[27] By "the Catholic moment" these writers refer to the relative coherence and unity of Catholic positions on such crucial issues as the economy, war and peace, social justice, and human rights. The issue, it seems to me, is mistakenly conceived of in terms of a static view of today's mainstream, assimilated U.S. Catholic. This mainstreamed Catholic church, educated and fairly affluent, is viewed as paradigmatic. But today's American Catholic context is anything but static. The Hispanic presence is one of the factors that make that context dynamic. Growing numbers of U.S. Catholics are neither mainstream nor affluent.

A related source of deformation is the controversy (using Joe Holland's terminology) among restorationists (conservatives), integrationists (liberals), and regenerationists (progressives). The regenerationist critique of the culture of modernity echoes similar concerns among Third World peoples like Hispanics. However, the interlocutors in this debate tend to be people firmly rooted in First World contexts. They lack, therefore, the kind of sensitivity that comes from real familiarity with other cultures. Consequently, the Hispanic perspective is once again absent from this debate. This points again to the tragic lack of intellectual voices among U.S. Hispanic Catholics and the inability of non-Hispanic Catholic thinkers to address the issues from various unique Hispanic viewpoints.

Similarly, something that has not contributed to the development of a strong Hispanic vision of the "American Catholic moment" is the controversy between American Catholic progressives (especially theologians and feminists) and Rome. It is not that this controversy has no merit. I do not want to belittle

27. Joe Holland and Anne Barsanti, eds., *American and Catholic: The New Debate* (South Orange, N.J.: Pillar Books, 1988).

the serious and worthy issues that are at stake. Rather, I wish to say that in some respects these issues are debated and expressed from the narrow point of view of First World interlocutors.[28] Ask Hispanics what they think about the burning issues reported in the *National Catholic Reporter* or debated in our theological academies, and the answers may be surprising. The Hispanic context and the reflection that rightly flows from it are characteristically absent. Our burning issues are not those of American Catholic academia, liberals, progressives, or conservatives, much less those of European integralists.[29]

Multiculturalism as Ideology

Another factor limiting the effectiveness of society's and the church's outreach to Hispanics is an unanalyzed assumption that cultural groups in a new and seemingly hostile milieu can simply be juxtaposed within a multicultural context without carefully providing them with a sense of their identity and security. Time and effort must be invested in nonmainstream cultures. They must be allowed to "do their thing," to have their own ministers and their own turf. These are the human means that experience should have taught us are indispensable if there is eventually to

28. A possible exception to the general lack of in-depth discussion of "the American Catholic moment" within theological circles is the issue of *New Theology Review*, vol. 2, no. 3, August 1989. This issue, edited by Robert J. Schreiter, is devoted to "The Marks of Being Catholic Today" and takes seriously black and Hispanic perspectives.

29. For a summary of issues of great importance to U.S. Hispanic theologians, see Allan Figueroa Deck, presidential address at the Second Annual Meeting of the Academy of Catholic Hispanic Theologians of the United States, Graduate Theological Union, August 1989 (unpublished). One point of contact between theology from a Hispanic perspective and mainstream theology is liberation theology, which has received a fair amount of attention. That theology, however, has so far been articulated in terms of non-U.S. Hispanics. Its methods and concerns have yet to be significantly applied "at home."

be unity. The rush toward the integration of the parish, for instance, creates situations of discomfort for the new immigrant groups as well as for the old-timers. The strong effective approach needed to attract and sustain Hispanics, real respect for their popular religiosity, and liturgy that they can identify with are hard if not impossible to pursue in many multicultural contexts. There are just too many different tastes and needs to satisfy. No wonder that Hispanics are being attracted to evangelical sects that have learned the lesson well: they organize Hispanic members into small communities and provide them with ministers—usually native Hispanics—who speak the people's lingo and come from the same socioeconomic class.[30]

Class or Culture?

Joseph Fitzpatrick has suggested that the issue of socioeconomic class is perhaps as important as or more important than the issue of cultural difference in assessing the current status of Hispanics in the U.S. Catholic church.[31] I think he is onto something. Historical and pastoral sensitivities in today's U.S. church are markedly middle-class. We have lost the strong blue-collar orientation of other times. That means that our "gut-level" interests and commitments are quite removed from those of working-class Hispanics. We must study the effect that this class orientation has on our priorities and interests. I am not aware of any straightforward analysis of this important change in American Catholicism. An analogy that I find interesting but

30. See Allan Figueroa Deck, S.J., "Proselytism and Hispanic Catholics," in *America*, 10 December 1988, 485–90; also Garardo Marín and Raymond J. Gamba, "Expectations and Experiences of Hispanic Catholics and Converts to Protestant Churches" (San Francisco: USF Social Psychology Laboratory Hispanic Studies, no. 2, 1990).

31. Joseph A. Fitzpatrick, S.J., "The Hispanic Poor in a Middle Class Church," (Bronx, N.Y.: Department of Sociology, Fordham University, 1986).

also somewhat alarming is with Episcopalianism. Is the Roman Catholic Church becoming more like the Episcopal church, that is, markedly middle-class and establishment? I suggest that such a trend means diminishment in numbers and a move away from the masses and from Hispanics and other minority groups in particular. This is a thorny and delicate issue that few if any are taking seriously.

Roger Finke and Rodney Stark have written a provocative piece on the process by which mainline Protestant churches have gone into decline by becoming strongly middle-class and "establishment."[32] Could the U.S. Catholic church be taking the same route? If Hispanics find a firm place in the church today, that decline will not take place. The jury is not yet in.

The Need for Leadership

Perhaps the most obvious conclusion that can be made about the Hispanic presence in the U.S. Catholic church is the need for an educated Hispanic Catholic leadership. I do not wish to belittle the Hispanic leaders that we have. I suppose I am one of them. But in all honesty it seems to me that there are not nearly enough of us. The absence of thinkers rooted in the experience of the people—organic intellectuals, as Antonio Gramsci would call them—is due perhaps to a certain attitude that has been called *basismo*. By *basismo* I mean the idea that the only legitimate reflections come from the grass-roots people themselves and that the "second moment" in the elaboration of theology and other reflections on the reality, the more scientific, scholarly, or systematic phases, are ipso facto suspect. Antonio Gramsci has stressed the essential role of intellectuals in the process of all socioeconomic and political transformations. Although elaborated within the framework of Marxist humanism,

32. Roger Finke and Rodney Stark, "How the Upstart Sects Won America: 1776–1850," *Journal for the Scientific Study of Religion* 28 (1989): 27–44.

his view highlights an integral vision of the human (body, mind, and spirit) that is at the heart of the gospel message we Catholics and Christians profess. Resistance to the role of the intellectual, or anti-intellectualism, contributes to the lack of a vigorous Hispanic presence in North American intellectual life where power and influence can be exercised for the common good.

The fact is that the reflections we U.S. Hispanics have been able to make remain relatively obscure, even paltry, in comparison to the magnitude of the challenge. I believe that is due, at least in part, because of our failure to cultivate Hispanic, organic intellectuals.[33] This is an urgent need. In light of this need the formation of the Academy of Hispanic Catholic Theologians of the United States (ACHTUS) must be seen as a promising, perhaps even historic, event.

The lack of Hispanic intellectuals in church and society is due largely to the failure of education, especially Catholic education, to rise to the challenge of the Hispanic presence. Catholic education succeeded admirably in educating many of our mainstream Catholics. This is to its everlasting glory. But, despite some important contributions to the education of Hispanics from kindergarten through college and graduate school, the picture is not good. As the Association of Theological Schools' *Fact Book on Theological Education 1987–88* indicates, Hispanic theological leadership is being developed much more among Protestants than among Roman Catholics.[34] Something similar is happening with respect to Catholic universities, which are trying to attract Hispanics and other minorities, but with limited success. Hispanic leaders are not being educated in Catholic institutions to nearly the same extent as was the case with other U.S. Catholic ethnic groups. Nothing short of a massive commitment of resources and a reordering of priorities will change

33. See Antonio Gramsci, *Gli intellettuale e l'organizzazione della cultura* (Turin: Editori Riuniti, 1979).
34. See note 15 above.

19

this situation. Such a reorientation, unfortunately, does not appear to be likely.

Consequently the Hispanic presence in the U.S. Catholic church will continue to languish, deprived of the articulation and depth that it requires if it is to emerge with all its strength and originality. Until that happens it will be extremely difficult to say what it really means to be Hispanic and Catholic in today's and tomorrow's United States of America. Yves Congar's vision of a world evangelized by today's marginalized peoples will be postponed until the dominant Euro-North American culture comes to grips with the limitations of its intellectual culture and with its prejudices and omissions based on its social location and self-interests.

This chapter has been an attempt to trace a general outline of issues that need to be addressed if the Hispanic presence is ever to enter into serious and sustained dialogue with the hegemonic, Euro-North American culture. The 1990 conference at Emory University represented an enormous contribution to that desperately needed dialogue insofar as it provided us with a deeper and more engaging articulation of what it means to be Hispanic, Catholic, and North American today. In so doing it contributed an essential ingredient in the creation of a new kind of North American culture for the twenty-first century, an era that may be the Hispanic century in United States history.

2

Hispanic American Theology and the Bible:
Effective Weapon and Faithful Ally

Fernando F. Segovia

Neither the task of theologizing nor the task of interpretation—both highly interrelated and interdependent activities—takes place in a social vacuum, independent of the social location, howsoever defined, of the theologian or interpreter in question. Such a theoretical position is by no means new, but it has come into much greater prominence, and with much greater vehemence, in the last quarter of this century than ever before. In this study I wish to explore the emerging readings of the Bible from within one such specific social location, namely that ethnic sector of American society generally referred to as the Hispanic Americans, a sector in which I stand and from which I speak.

FERNANDO F. SEGOVIA

The Standpoint of Hispanic American Theology

The Question of Social Location

In modern times the relationship between social location and the theological or interpretive enterprise has always been tacitly admitted, if not always explicitly addressed and analyzed, in the theological disciplines. For the most part, however, such a relationship has been acknowledged in terms of religious or church affiliation. Thus, for example, it is not at all uncommon to speak of Orthodox theology, Catholic theology, Lutheran theology, or evangelical theology. Similarly, at a fundamental level of religious training and socialization, religious bodies—across the full spectrum of ideological position and ecclesiastical polity— have always insisted on the theological education of their ordained ministry and religious leadership within the boundaries of their own confessional settings, properly separated—with the distance in question differently conceived and postulated by the different bodies—from the educational settings of other churches and with the boundaries between such settings properly defined and regulated.

Even in the present age of ecumenism, nondenominational seminaries or divinity schools have remained few in number. A decided preference for denominational seminaries is still very much at work and seemingly on the rise across the ecclesiastical spectrum, even among those religious bodies that do in principle grant the concept and practice of theological education in an ecumenical setting. A confessional setting is still perceived throughout as the most adequate way of insuring the preservation and continuation of a religious tradition at a multidimensional level, encompassing in fact the whole ethos of a religious body: its self-understanding and ideology; its reading of history and tradition; its polity and praxis; its theological canon—what is to be read and by whom is it written; as well as its reading or interpretive strategy with regard to the Bible—

22

which theoretical orientation is to be adopted and which methodological procedures are to be followed.

In the last fifteen years or so, however, the theological disciplines have begun to witness a radical expansion of the concept of social location and hence a radical shift in the understanding of the relationship between the social location of the theologian or interpreter and the task of theologizing or interpretation. In effect, social location is no longer perceived primarily in terms of religious affiliation but rather in terms of a highly complex matrix of identity factors; as a result, the relationship between social location and theologizing or interpretation is now seen as much more complex as well, with any one of these factors, or any combination thereof, subject to critical study and analysis. In fact, as a result of such a shift, the theological disciplines are becoming much more nondenominational or ecumenical than the religious bodies are, insofar as these other identity factors ultimately cut across all religious bodies.

Thus, from the beginning of the 1970s, theological studies have seen the explosion of a number of movements that have called into question the established theological methods, with their often implicit claims to universality and objectivity. Similarly, the end of the 1970s witnessed the displacement of the long-reigning and universally accepted paradigm of historical criticism within biblical studies, with its implicit search for a sole, definitive, and objective meaning of the biblical text—a meaning that was usually located in either the world represented by the text or in the intention of the author of the text. Both of these shifts were fundamental in character, involving profound and far-reaching theoretical and methodological changes.

In the field of theological studies, this shift was in part represented by a deliberate and explicit attention to the role of context in the theological task, with a wide variety of contextual theologies emerging as a result; for example, liberation theologies of the Third World, feminist theology, and so-called minority theologies of the First World.[1] In the field of biblical studies, this shift was characterized by a full turn to both social criticism, involving a wide range of the theoretical spectrum (e.g., sectarianism, millenarianism, social dynamics and roles, sociology of knowledge, Mediterranean studies), and literary criticism, again covering a wide range of the theoretical spectrum (e.g., narratology, rhetorical theory, communications theory, feminist criticism, reader response).[2] While sociological and anthropological methodologies have emphasized the social location of the biblical texts (with some attention given as well to the social location of the readers of such texts), literary methodologies have brought out not only the rhetorical and ideological character of the texts as such but also the complex nature of the act of reading and interpretation, with reader response criticism, given its focus on the reader and on meaning as a process of negotiation between text and reader, gaining increasing momentum in the discipline through the 1980s.[3]

1. For a good and succinct account of this change, see Susan Brooks Thistlethwaite and Mary Potter Engel, "Introduction: Making the Connections Among Liberation Theologies Around the World," in *Lift Every Voice: Constructing Theologies from the Underside*, eds. Thistlethwaite and Engel (San Francisco: Harper & Row, 1990), 1–15.

2. For good and succinct accounts of these developments, see Mark Allan Powell, *What Is Narrative Criticism?* (Guides to Biblical Scholarship; Minneapolis: Fortress Press, 1990), esp. 1–21; Bruce J. Malina, "The Social Sciences and Biblical Interpretation," *Interpretation* 36 (1981): 229–42; and "Why Interpret the Bible with the Social Sciences?" *American Baptist Quarterly* 2 (1983): 119–33.

3. For introductions to reader response criticism, see, e.g., Susan Suleiman, "Introduction: Varieties of Audience-Oriented Criticism," in *The Reader in the Text: Essays on Audience and Interpretation*, eds. Suleiman and Inge Crosman (Princeton, N.J.: Princeton University Press, 1980), 3–45; Jane P. Tompkins, "An Introduction to Reader-Response Criticism," in *Reader-Response Criticism: From Formalism to Post-Structuralism*, ed. Tompkins (Baltimore and London: Johns Hopkins University Press, 1980), ix–xxvi; Elizabeth Freund, *The Return of the Reader: Reader-Response Criticism* (New Accents; London and New York: Methuen, 1987), esp. 1–20 ("Introduction: The Order of Reading"). For reader response criticism in biblical studies, see Robert

In both cases, therefore, a distinct shift in orientation can be observed: away from largely implicit claims to objectivity and universality, toward an explicit and critical focus on the theologian or interpreter and his or her social location. In other words, the issue of standpoint or perspective has come fully to the fore in the theological disciplines, with the theological or interpretive task now seen as directly shaped or influenced by the social location of the individual in question; as a result, certain factors traditionally left out of consideration have now become an important focus of critical attention as well—gender, racial background, ethnic background, socioeconomic class, sociopolitical status and allegiance, sociocultural conventions, educational levels, ideological position, as well as religious affiliation.

The Hispanic American Social Location

In this study I focus on Hispanic Americans as a distinct and identifiable configuration of social location, specifically circumscribed in terms of both ethnic background and sociopolitical status, and on the readings of the Bible that are beginning to emerge out of this group. Some preliminary observations are in order with respect to the configuration as such.

(1) The issue of nomenclature is complex and should be approached with care, subject to ongoing revision. I use the term Hispanic American to designate those individuals of Hispanic descent, associated in one way or another with the Americas (South, Central, North, and the Caribbean), who now live permanently, for whatever reason, in the United States of America.

On the one hand, the question of ethnic background is paramount in the designation. First, to be "of Hispanic descent" means to have, at least in part, a physical and/or cultural Spanish

Detweiler, ed., *Reader Response Approaches to Biblical and Secular Texts*, *Semeia* 31 (Decatur, Ga.: Scholars Press, 1985).

heritage, with language as an important unifying force in this regard.[4] Second, to be "associated in one way or another with the Americas" means to have a direct or indirect connection with the former colonies of Spain rather than with the European colonial power as such.[5] On the other hand, the question of sociopolitical status is also essential to the designation. First, to live "permanently in the United States" means to do so either as citizens, born or naturalized, or as residents, legal or illegal. Second, the phrase "for whatever reason" means that the basis for such permanent residence in the United States may be political, economic, territorial, or any combination thereof.

(2) This terminology is not only complex but also problematic, subject to much discussion among Hispanic Americans themselves. Members of the group hail from many different quarters and many different cultures, always identifying themselves in terms of their country of origin, whether immediate (as in the case of immigrants) or remote (as in the case of later generations or those born in territories annexed by the United States). Thus, the terms that are usually employed to distinguish the group as a whole within the United States—*Latinos* or *Hispanics*—are not terms that the group uses of itself, but rather terms that have been applied to the group by the dominant

4. To be sure, many Hispanic Americans have, at least in part, a physical African and/or native heritage, while all share, to one degree or another, such a cultural heritage as well. It is this rich and creative racial and cultural mixture that gives rise to the important notion of *mestizaje* in Hispanic American thought and theology.

5. Immigrants, most of whom come to the United States already fully socialized within their own respective countries of origin, have a direct relationship. Their children, whether born in this country or brought at an early age, have an indirect connection, with the full process of socialization taking place in this country. In addition, there are Hispanic Americans whose homeland was annexed by the United States, whether in the continental mainland or in Puerto Rico; these have a direct connection as well, most pronounced in Puerto Rico. For Hispanic Americans in this latter category, the term *immigrant* is not at all proper—it was not they who came to the United States, but the United States who came to them.

culture of the country. Such terms, furthermore, are used more often than not in a highly misinformed and misleading fashion, insofar as they carry not only a presumption of undifferentiated sameness, though we are very different (despite our profound similarities) from one another, but also a distinct racial connotation, though the group as a whole encompasses a number of different races, following the more traditional (supposedly biological) understanding of this term.[6]

I prefer the term *Hispanic American* on several counts. First, such a designation emphasizes via the adjective *Hispanic* the connection with Spain, distinguishing us thereby from other groups in the Americas with a different colonial heritage, such as Brazil (Portugal); Haiti, French Guiana, and a number of Caribbean islands (France); the Bahamas, Jamaica, and other Caribbean islands (England); Surinam and other Caribbean islands (Holland).[7] Second, such a designation also emphasizes by way of the noun *American* the present and permanent connection of the group with the United States. Finally, the designation follows common parlance with regard to ethnic descent in the United States, where such designations as "Irish American" and "Italian American" are common, though in our case the term can only be used (as, for example, in the similar case of Arab Americans) as an umbrella term encompassing a wide variety of different subgroups, such as Mexican Americans, Puerto Ricans, and Cuban Americans. To be sure, the designation does have drawbacks: it is not a term for which we are

---

6. For different and changing understandings of "race," see Michael Banton, *Racial and Ethnic Competition* (Comparative Ethnic and Race Relations Series; Cambridge: Cambridge University Press, 1983), 32–59; Joe R. Feagin, *Racial and Ethnic Relations* (Englewood Cliffs, N.J.: Prentice-Hall, 1978), 4–19.

7. There are other groups in the Americas with a different European heritage, such as German or Italian, especially in the southernmost countries of South America; however, the colonial heritage within which they find themselves is still that of Spain, with the Spanish language as a unifying force once again. Not many Hispanic Americans trace their roots to such groups.

directly responsible, nor is it a term that embodies in itself, given its English formulation, our distinctive linguistic heritage.

(3) The group as a whole has experienced phenomenal growth in the last two decades—a 53 percent increase from 1980 to 1990 alone—largely as a result of continuing immigration and a higher than average birthrate. Thus, whereas the projected figures for the 1990 census ranged from a lowest estimate of 19.15 million to a highest estimate of 22.05 million, the preliminary figures recently released by the Census Bureau show a count of 22.4 million, well beyond the highest estimate and probably subject to serious undercounting as well.[8] As a group, therefore, Hispanic Americans presently account for 9 percent to 10 percent of the total population of the country, with figures surpassing the 25 percent mark in some states (New Mexico, California, Texas). Their presence in the country is clearly significant and on the increase; in fact, it is estimated that by the end of the century Hispanic Americans will have become the largest minority group in the country.

(4) At the same time, from both a socioeconomic and educational point of view, the group as a whole shows a considerable lag with respect to the rest of the population. This is true of such economic indexes as median income, unemployment, business ownership, and home ownership; in fact, approximately 23 percent of Hispanic Americans were found to be living in poverty in 1990, as defined by government figures. It is also true of educational attainment at all levels, from primary school to university; the dropout rate among Hispanic Americans is close to a truly alarming 35 percent.[9] In addition, from a sociopolitical point of view, political representation has remained

8. For projections, see U.S. Department of Commerce, Bureau of the Census, *Population Estimates and Projections*, ser. P-25, no. 995. For a preliminary report on the actual figures, see Felicity Barringer, "Census Shows Profound Change in Racial Makeup of the Nation," *New York Times*, 11 March 1991; for undercounting, see Barringer, "Census Revisions Would Widen Political Gains of Three Big States," *New York Times*, 14 June 1991.

9. For a brief but informative overview, see Justo L. González, *The*

meager and ineffective, a definite drawback within the American political system. Despite its significant presence and growth in American society, therefore, the group's overall situation has remained marginal.

(5) Despite their divergent backgrounds and natural tendency to define themselves in terms of their country of origin, Hispanic Americans have more recently begun to see themselves as a distinctive group with common needs and goals, with a specific and urgent agenda, within the American political and cultural scene.[10] To be sure, their social situation of marginalization as well as the general tenor of outside reaction toward the group, marked by widespread and sustained discrimination, have played a key role in this regard. This same development of conscientization and consolidation within the group may also be seen at work in the American theological scene. In effect, the theological voice of Hispanic Americans has begun to make itself heard as a new and ironic kind of manifest destiny, from many different quarters but with many fundamental themes in common.[11] Not surprisingly, given the social picture outlined

---

Theological Education of Hispanics (New York: Fund for Theological Education, 1988), 9–16. See also Julie Johnson, "Hispanic Dropout Rate Is Put at 35 Percent," *New York Times*, 15 September 1989; Lawrence K. Altman, "Many Hispanic Americans Reported in Ill Health and Lacking Insurance," *New York Times*, 9 January 1991; Felicity Barringer, "Hispanic Americans Gain but Still Lag Economically, Report Says," *New York Times*, 11 April 1991.

10. See, e.g., Richard Lacayo, "A Surging New Spirit," *Time*, 11 July 1988: 46–49; "Hispanic Role Set Out for '92 Election," *New York Times*, 27 September 1990; Seth Mydans, "California Expects Hispanic Voters to Transform Politics," *New York Times*, 27 January 1991.

11. For a critical overview, see Fernando F. Segovia, "A New Manifest Destiny: The Emerging Theological Voice of Hispanic Americans," *Religious Studies Review* 17 (1991): 101–9. See also John P. Rossing, "*Mestizaje* and Marginality: A Hispanic American Theology," *Theology Today* 45 (1988): 293–304, and José David Rodríguez, "De 'apuntes' a 'esbozo': diez años de reflexión," *Apuntes* 10 (1990): 75–83. For the theological voice of Puerto Ricans in Puerto Rico, see the interesting study by Luis N. Rivera Pagán, *Senderos teológicos: El pensamiento evangélico puertorriqueño* (Río Piedras, Puerto Rico: Editorial La Reforma, 1989).

above and the general reaction on the part of the dominant culture, such a voice has opted for the optic and methodology of liberation theology. As in the case of any theological stance, implicit or explicit, such a choice has had a direct effect on the way the Bible is used and read in Hispanic American theology. In what follows I shall trace such usage in the work of four Hispanic American theologians who represent a variety of ethnic and religious sectors, thereby bringing to light, in a broad comparative fashion, the reading strategies adopted with regard to the Bible from within such a distinct social location. I would describe my task at this point as critically descriptive rather than constructive, as a necessary first step in my own development of a Hispanic American hermeneutics.

Hispanic American Theology and the Bible

Mujerista *Theology and the Bible: Ada María Isasi-Díaz*

There are still, regrettably, few female Hispanic American theologians; Ada María Isasi-Díaz, a Cuban American and Roman Catholic, has been by far the best known and the most active in theological circles. Her work, which comes out of an explicitly feminist perspective, has been concerned throughout with the development of a liberation theology for Hispanic American women, a theology she has recently begun to call *mujerista* theology.[12] Although for the most part the Bible has

---

12. The term *mujerista* is a new adjective formed from the noun *mujer*, "woman," and referring to whatever contributes to the liberation of Hispanic American women. For the main formulation of such a theology, see Ada María Isasi-Díaz's volume, coauthored with Yolanda Tarango, *Hispanic Women: Prophetic Voice in the Church* (San Francisco: Harper & Row, 1988). For the gradual development of this theology and the terminology involved, see " '*Apuntes*' for a Hispanic Women's Theology of Liberation," *Apuntes* 6 (1986): 61–71; "Toward an Understanding of *Feminismo Hispano* in the U.S.A.," in *Women's Consciousness, Women's Conscience: A Reader in Feminist Ethics,* ed. Barbara H. Andolsen, Christine E. Gudorf, and Mary D. Pellauer (New York: Winston,

been of minimal importance in her work, she has recently turned her attention for the first time to the question of a proper use of and role for the Bible in *mujerista* theology.[13] Although such reflections are still in progress at this point, I include them in this overview, given the crucial importance of the gender factor in contemporary theological thinking.

Mujerista theology is but one application of a much wider movement described as the struggle of Hispanic American women to liberate themselves not as individuals but as members of a community, with a radical vision of justice and peace in mind. As such, *mujerista* theology, like the wider movement itself, has as its point of departure the experience of Hispanic American women in an Anglo-Saxon dominant culture, facing oppression from both a sexist world (as women) and a racist world (as Hispanic), with a specific focus on such oppression within religious systems. *Mujerista* theology is defined, therefore, as a liberative praxis, a reflective action that has as its goal liberation; its basic parameters are described as follows. First,

---

1985), 51–61; "A Hispanic Garden in a Foreign Land," in *Inheriting Our Mothers' Gardens*, ed. Letty Russell et al. (Philadelphia: Westminster Press, 1988), 91–106; "*Mujeristas*: A Name of Our Own," *The Christian Century*, 24 May 1989, 560-62; "*Mujeristas*: A Name of Our Own," in *The Future of Liberation Theology: Essays in Honor of Gustavo Gutiérrez*, ed. Marc H. Ellis and Otto Maduro (Maryknoll, N.Y.: Orbis Books, 1989) 410–19; "Hispanic in America," *Christianity and Crisis*, 13 May 1991, 150–52; and Ada María Isasi-Díaz, "*Mujeristas* and *Mujerismo*: Who We Are and What We Are About," *Journal of Feminist Studies of Religion* (Spring 1992).

13. Ada María Isasi-Díaz, "The Bible and *Mujerista* Theology," in Thisthlethwaite and Engel, *Lift Every Voice*, 261–69. It should be pointed out— and this is a fundamental weakness of *mujerista* theology as presently conceived and formulated—that this theology has a distinct, if not exclusive, Roman Catholic context in mind, namely, the experience of Hispanic American women of Roman Catholic background. Indeed, it would be interesting to see what a *mujerista* theology emerging out of the growing Protestant tradition would look like, especially with regard to biblical hermeneutics. On Protestant women and the Bible, see Mary Ann Tolbert, "Protestant Feminists and the Bible: On the Horns of a Dilemma," *Union Seminary Quarterly Review* 43 (1989): 1–17.

it does not differentiate between reflection and action, theology and ethics. Second, it does not operate out of the interpretive lens of a patriarchal church but rather out of the experiential norm of Hispanic American women. Third, it is not sectarian but communal in character. Finally, it has survival as its primary goal. Such survival is portrayed in terms of liberation rather than equality, with the following specific aims in mind: a radical change in the oppressive structures of society; conscientization regarding the profound internalization of such oppressive structures, with individual conversion as a necessary first step; and an eschatological vision of a new society.

Within *mujerista* theology the Bible is seen as playing a very important though limited role. On the one hand, given the peripheral role of the Bible in the religious lives of Hispanic American women, there is a call for an explicit recovery and incorporation of the biblical texts as a central element in *mujerista* theology.[14] Such a call is grounded on a variety of reasons, ranging from the theological to the political: (1) biblical tradition as not only playing an indirect role in the lives of Hispanic American women as Christians but also as in fundamental accord with the core values of justice and love in their own popular religiosity; (2) the liturgical and instructional changes introduced by Vatican II; (3) the importance of the Bible in the ethos of the dominant culture; (4) the Bible as an effective weapon in the

---

14. The reasons for the peripheral role of the Bible are important. First, the Christianity of the Spanish *conquista* (conquest) was not a biblical Christianity but rather a Christianity tied to the doctrines, commandments, and practices of the church. The Christianity of Hispanic American women is the Christianity of popular religiosity, a mixture or *mestizaje* of this nonbiblical religion of the *conquista* and the beliefs and practices of African and Amerindian religions. Second, in the popular religiosity of Hispanic American women, the figures of the saints have a much more prominent role than that of Jesus: while the saints are beyond the control of the official church and open to creative *mestizaje*, Jesus is seen as both belonging to the world of the church and as a male in a male-dominated culture. Third, the Bible is regarded as both difficult to understand and subject to the interpretation of the church.

daily struggle of Hispanic American women for survival. On the other hand, within *mujerista* theology the Bible remains ultimately subordinate to the experiential norm of Hispanic American women. It is to be accepted as normative and authoritative only insofar as it contributes to their struggle for survival and liberation; consequently, only those parts of the Bible that allow for the liberative praxis of Hispanic American women are accepted as revelatory and salvific.

In *mujerista* theology, therefore, one finds at work the common principle of a canon within the canon, with a twist: only parts of the Bible are accepted as normative and authoritative; such parts, moreover, are so judged on the basis of a superior canon—a feminist, Hispanic, liberative canon.[15] In effect, while the program of liberation has urgent need of the Bible, the Bible itself is seen as subject to the program of liberation. Thus, the Bible emerges as both liberating and oppressive, with the canon within the canon determined from the outside.

Barrio Theology and the Bible: Harold J. Recinos

Harold Recinos, a United Methodist minister and Puerto Rican born in New York City, has engaged in what can be best described as a critical exercise in pastoral theology from the perspective of liberation, a theology of and for the barrio.[16]

---

15. For a typology of feminist responses to the Bible, see Mary Ann Tolbert, "Defining the Problem: The Bible and Feminist Hermeneutics," in *The Bible and Feminist Hermeneutics*, ed. Tolbert, *Semeia* 28 (Chico, Calif.: Scholars Press, 1983), 113-26. The canon within the canon position adopted by Isasi-Díaz represents one of the three main types of responses.

16. Harold J. Recinos, *Hear the Cry! A Latino Pastor Challenges the Church* (Louisville: Westminster/John Knox Press, 1989). The basic meaning of the Spanish word barrio is simply that of "neighborhood," a circumscribed and recognized location within a city; to be sure, given the lack of mobility in our countries, barrios have a much more distinctive and permanent corporate personality. In the United States the word has also acquired the more specific denotation of "ghetto" or "inner city," meaning that neighborhood where the poor and the marginalized live and are condemned to live. Among its semantic

Within such a theology, the reading of the Bible emerges as the cornerstone of liberation, given the fundamental correspondence posited between the people of the barrio and the people of God in the Bible, the God of the Bible and the God of the barrio.

The point of departure for such a theology is quite concrete: the sociocultural situation of the large Puerto Rican communities who live in the barrios of northeastern U.S. cities (with New York City as the primary example) and its disastrous and lasting consequences for the countless individual lives in question, including the author's. This point of departure is ultimately generalized as well: the situation of the barrio as characteristic of the vast majority of Hispanic Americans in the United States, regardless of national origin or geographic location. For Recinos, the situation of the group is directly and inevitably replicated in the lives of its individual members. The barrio is faced with a dehumanizing situation akin to apartheid and marked by racial discrimination, cultural aggression, political marginalization, and economic oppression. Given such systemic conditions, the people of the barrio find themselves overwhelmed by a host of social ills, from inordinately high levels of poverty and unemployment to widespread crime and violence, ultimately yielding a profound attitude of self-blame and fatalism.[17] A theology of the barrio, therefore, is a theology that has in mind survival in the sense of liberation. For Recinos, such a theology is a theology that works, at both the personal and community levels, as he readily attests on the basis of his own personal and pastoral experience in the barrio.[18]

---

equivalents would be, for example, the *favela* (Brazil), the *arrabal* (Puerto Rico), the *tugurio* (Central America)—whatever can be described as a shantytown anywhere in the world.

17. For a good description of precisely such a situation in the city of Bridgeport, Connecticut, see Alan Weisman, "Unsettled, Unseen, Unspoken For: A Puerto Rican Community Finds Its Dreams Stranded in a Yankee Town," *New York Times Sunday Magazine*, 28 April 1991, 50.

18. For a similar social analysis of the urban Puerto Rican communities

A theology of the barrio, then, is a theology that seeks to make sense of the reality of oppression and to restore a sense of human dignity to the community and its members, with a vision of a new world based on justice and equality. Its basic parameters are further described as follows. First, barrio theology interprets the otherworldly character of the kingdom of God in terms of the present structures of injustice and inequality in the world; it is a theology that sees the kingdom as pointing to a world based on justice and equality. Second, barrio theology calls for a commitment to an active struggle against and a fundamental revision of all dehumanizing structures; it is a theology that must be accompanied by social, economic, and political analysis leading to social empowerment and change. Third, barrio theology also calls for both cooperation and confrontation in the struggle for liberation; it is a theology that must establish ties with theologies of the Third World and minority theologies within the country as well as issue a challenge to the theologies of the dominant culture. Finally, barrio theology opts for a new reading of the Bible similar to that of the Christian base communities of Latin America, an explicit reading from the perspective of the oppressed; it is a theology that reappropriates the basic story of the Bible: a God of the cross who identifies with the oppressed and the poor and who participates actively in their liberation.

At the heart of barrio theology, therefore, lies the Bible and, more specifically, a particular reading of the Bible. For Recinos such a reading of the Bible comes from the perspective of the poor, in effect from the perspective of the barrio, and yields a recovery of biblical Christianity: not only the realization that the sociocultural story of the barrio is shared by the people of God in the Bible, but also the discovery of a God who sides

and theological program of liberation, again with the Bible at its core, see David Traverzo, "Towards a Theology of Mission in the U.S. Puerto Rican Migrant Community: From Captivity to Liberation," *Apuntes* 9 (1989): 51–59.

with the marginalized, with the barrio, and works for their liberation. For Recinos this option of God for the poor and the oppressed is present in the law, with the exodus story as its creative center; it figures prominently in the prophetic tradition; it lies at the very heart of Jesus' proclamation of the kingdom; and it remains at the center of the Christian message during the first century of the church. It is only with the gradual accommodation of the church to imperial society in the second through fourth centuries that such a *prophetic* theology is displaced by a *royal* theology, giving rise to a theological tension present in the church ever since. Consequently, the reading of the Bible from the perspective of the marginalized, of the barrio, constitutes a return to and recovery of the fundamental message of the Bible.

For barrio theology, therefore, the Bible is indeed central and authoritative. Its message throughout, in both Old and New Testaments, is one of liberation: God is with the poor and for the poor. However, such a message demands a specific kind of reading, an open and explicit reading from the perspective of the oppressed, from a sociocultural situation parallel to that of the people of God in the Bible and with liberation in mind. Thus, the liberation of the barrio is grounded in and informed by the Bible: the program of liberation is ultimately the program of the Bible itself.

Mestizaje *Theology and the Bible: Virgilio Elizondo*

Certainly the most active voice in Hispanic American theology has been that of Virgilio Elizondo, a Roman Catholic priest of Mexican American extraction. Out of his own personal and pastoral experience in the borderlands of the American Southwest, Elizondo has developed what he calls a theology of *mestizaje*, a theology of liberation for Mexican Americans based on the principle of racial and cultural inclusion, on the richness of racial and cultural mixture.[19] For such a theology it is the

19. The basic meaning of the word *mestizaje* is that of racial miscegenation

concrete sociocultural situation of Jesus himself as preserved in the Gospels that is central and authoritative, insofar as Jesus, given his own origins as a mestizo from the borderlands of Galilee and his message of universal inclusion, anticipates the situation and liberation of Mexican Americans.

The theology of *mestizaje* finds its point of departure in the Mexican American experience of the borderlands between the United States and Mexico: a mestizo community with a twofold historical experience of conquest from the outside, first by the Spanish Catholic and then by the Nordic Protestant, and a bi-cultural identity, equally at home in Mexico and in the United States but fully at home in neither. For Elizondo such a sociohistorical and sociocultural situation of *mestizaje*, of the Mexican American as insider-outsider, yields both the harsh reality of marginalization and the key to liberation; in fact, it is only through an open and explicit appropriation of such marginalization that liberation can take place.

On the one hand, as a mestizo group, Mexican Americans are regarded by the dominant culture of North America as inferior, impure, underdeveloped, uncivilized. Such an attitude has led to pervasive and enduring marginalization at all levels of society. Mexican Americans are also regarded as different by Mexican culture, though by no means with the same degree of rejection and contempt as in North American culture. On the other hand, as a mestizo group, Mexican Americans find themselves in the privileged position of knowing their parent cultures, the dominant culture of the country as well as Mexican culture, better than they know themselves—from within and without.

---

between the white colonizers of Spain and the colonized indigenous population of the Americas; by extension the term also refers to any type of mixture, such as linguistic or cultural, involving these two or indeed any other "races." For the background and elaboration of such a theology, see Virgilio Elizondo, *Mestizaje: The Dialectic of Birth and Gospel* (San Antonio: Mexican American Cultural Center, 1978); *Galilean Journey* and *The Future Is Mestizo*. For a similar approach from the Puerto Rican experience, see Caleb Rosado, "Thoughts on a Puerto Rican Theology of Community," *Apuntes* 9 (1989): 10–12.

As a result, they can engage not only in sharp cultural critique but also in constructive cultural formation, rejecting the worst and choosing the best of both sides and thus serving as a bridge of understanding between two peoples. In other words, it is precisely their situation of *mestizaje* that can allow them to develop a liberating edge in the midst of their profound marginalization—a rich, critical biculturalism.

Such a critical edge lies at the heart of *mestizaje* theology: it is a theology characterized by a fundamental search for identity leading to conscientization and liberation. *Mestizaje* theology entails sociocultural conscientization: first, a rediscovery of cultural origins and a full appropriation of such origins, of biculturalism, in the face of widespread racism; second, an active commitment, as a bicultural community, to social confrontation and change in the light of severe marginalization and discrimination—political, economic, educational, and religious. Thus, with the recovery of cultural identity comes a program of social critique and empowerment. At the same time, *mestizaje* theology does not seek union and assimilation but rather liberation for all: it looks upon *mestizaje* as a source of enormous richness and vitality; it accepts the suffering and rejection of *mestizaje* as a point of departure for its own message of love and inclusion; and it works out of a vision of an expanding global *mestizaje* leading to a celebration of diversity and a new life for humanity.

For Elizondo this theology, like any other Christian theology, must be rooted in and judged by the word of the gospel. Thus, all local expressions of the faith, historically and culturally conditioned as they are, must be in fundamental accord with the original and normative experience of the faith present in the tradition of the church, above all in the writings of the New Testament and especially in the Gospels. Such accord involves a basic principle of correspondence: the function of Jesus in relation to his own history and culture provides the essential parameters for his function in any local expression of the faith or the gospel; otherwise, any concrete expression of the faith may be substituted for *the* faith and any concrete expression of the gospel may displace *the* gospel. To be sure, Elizondo sees *mestizaje* theology as eminently in accord with both faith and gospel: Jesus himself was a fellow mestizo with a similar program and vision of inclusion as liberation. This program of liberation is described in terms of three major geographical stages in the life of Jesus, each of which gives rise to a corresponding theological principle: the experience in Galilee, the fulfillment in Jerusalem, and the movement beyond all borders.[20] First, the Galilean ministry reveals a place of *mestizaje* giving rise to a message of inclusion in Israel that breaks down all barriers—all are one in the family of God. This message, however, goes beyond all expectations and provokes a crisis. Second, the journey to Jerusalem involves confrontation with the establishment and the unmasking of the system, with the crisis leading to suffering and death. Third, the resurrection appearances unfold a new way of life and liberation, involving the breakdown of all exclusions and a message of universal inclusion, so that in the end the crisis results in total victory. Thus, the message of Jesus is seen as a message of a mestizo from a place of *mestizaje*: a message of inclusion and rejoicing in diversity in the kingdom of God.

As in the case of *mujerista* theology, therefore, one can see in *mestizaje* theology the principle of the canon within the canon at work once again, but with fundamental differences in application. Here, the Bible is not subject to a superior canon, but rather a specific strand within the Bible is singled out as the superior canon. Likewise, the Bible is not judged liberating and authoritative from the outside, but rather the Bible itself, as authoritative and liberating in the light of this canon, passes

20. For a similar use of these geographical stages in the life of Jesus, from the point of view of contemporary evangelization, see Orlando Costas, *Liberating News: A Theology of Contextual Evangelization* (Grand Rapids, Mich.: Wm. B. Eerdmans, 1989), 49–70 (chap. 4: "The Evangelistic Legacy of Jesus: A Perspective from the Galilean Periphery").

judgment from within. This superior canon is identified in terms of the Gospels, though it would be more accurate to say that it is the Synoptic Gospels that Elizondo has in mind; in fact, for Elizondo the canon consists of the Synoptic Gospels insofar as they faithfully reproduce the life of Jesus of Nazareth. In other words, the superior canon is ultimately the life of the historical Jesus as preserved in the Synoptic Gospels. Moreover, the overall pattern of this life grounds and validates any proper Christian theology, with three basic moments yielding three fundamental theological principles: the Galilean principle of inclusion—God chooses what human beings reject; the Jerusalem principle of confrontation—the chosen rejected have a God-given mission to society; and the resurrection principle of universal inclusion— God brings new life out of suffering and death.

For *mestizaje* theology, therefore, the situation and liberation of Mexican Americans are anticipated in the life and message of the Galilean mestizo: God is with and for mestizos, actively working for inclusion and liberation in the world. Mexican Americans stand among the chosen rejected and can point the way to the new universalism and new life inaugurated by and in Jesus.

Mañana *Theology and the Bible: Justo L. González*

While the three preceding theological visions find their point of departure in different social configurations within the Hispanic American reality (women; Puerto Ricans in the barrios; Mexican Americans in the borderlands of the Southwest), the work of Justo González, a Cuban American and minister of the United Methodist Church, is concerned with the development of a theology of liberation for the group as a whole, what he calls a theology of *mañana* for all Hispanic Americans, in line with a new reformation at work in the contemporary Christian world.[21] As a central element of this theology, González provides

21. The Spanish word *mañana* means "tomorrow." In direct and ironic

what is by far the most explicit and self-conscious discussion of a proper biblical hermeneutics for Hispanic Americans, what he calls a reading "in Spanish."[22]

González sees *mañana* theology as having a twofold point of departure. First, it finds a concrete point of departure in the sociocultural situation of Hispanic Americans as a people "in exile": a people both alien, living in a land that, regardless of origins or status, does not acknowledge them as its own; and powerless, facing, as the statistics sharply point out, pronounced marginalization and discrimination in every segment of society. Second, it also finds a broader point of departure in the global coalescence of certain historical and political developments ultimately informing the new reformation under way in the church: (1) the displacement of the traditional and entrenched theology of glory, with its support for the existing order of society, by a theology of the cross, with a commitment to social change and transformation; (2) the evident failure of the many promises and panaceas of the Northern hemisphere, whether of the East or the West; and (3) the growing voice of the vast multitudes of the world that had remained silent until now. *Mañana* theology has its point of departure, therefore, among Hispanic Americans, within the Northern hemisphere, as one of these previously silent groups now coming to the fore with a vision of liberation in mind.

Thus, for González *mañana* theology represents the theology of a people "in exile": a people who will be around for many

---

contrast to its common usage by the dominant culture to describe Hispanic Americans as fundamentally lazy—what could be called the *mañana*-is-good-enough-for-me syndrome—González employs the term as pointing to a vision of a different tomorrow and a radical questioning of today.

22. See Justo L. González, *Mañana: Christian Theology from a Hispanic Perspective* (Nashville: Abingdon Press, 1990). With his wife, Catherine Gunsalus González, he has also been at work in the development of both a homiletics and a liturgics of liberation: *Liberation Preaching: The Pulpit and the Oppressed* (Nashville: Abingdon Press, 1980); *In Accord: Let Us Worship* (New York: Friendship Press, 1981).

mañanas to come; who hope for an altogether different *mañana* in the light of God's reign; and who engage in a radical questioning of today in the light of this coming *mañana*, this good news of a new creation. *Mañana* theology is not, therefore, the theology of the proverbially lazy and underdeveloped, but rather the theology of an alien and disadvantaged minority that suffers and struggles. As such, it has much in common with the dominant theological vision behind the new reformation: (1) an understanding of truth in concrete historical terms, in terms of peace and justice—its goal is social change and transformation; (2) a radical ecumenism, with a focus on orthopraxis as the way to union—it encompasses both Catholic and Protestant Hispanic Americans; and (3) a rejection of North Atlantic theology as universal and normative, with an explicit option for contextual and concrete theology—it grows out of the community and has the community constantly in mind. Thus, *mañana* theology emerges as a communal, contextual, ecumenical theology of liberation.

Within such a theological vision the Bible occupies a central and authoritative position. At the same time, *mañana* theology calls for a specific way of reading the Bible, a reading in the vernacular, "in Spanish"—a reading that is beyond innocence, from a people painfully aware of its own noninnocent identity and history; a reading from the perspective of exile, from an alien and disadvantaged people called to new life by God; and a reading that is naive but not simplistic, from a people not afraid to lay claim to its own reading and to insert itself fully into biblical history. This reading "in Spanish" is ultimately a reading of resistance and hence a reading of subversion.

First, such a reading is noninnocent insofar as it resists any type of innocent and comfortable idealization of history. It does not presuppose high ideals, purity, and perfection throughout, thereby engaging in a highly selective reading of the Bible; rather, it openly acknowledges the many skeletons present in the closets of the biblical protagonists, whether of the Old or

New Testaments (including Jesus himself). It looks to the God of history, who chooses such people for his plans, and history itself, which keeps moving despite highly unlikely channels as well as continuous and radical failures, for its only heroes. As such, it is a reading of the Bible that emerges from a people fully aware of its own painful beginnings, a reading in search of a common acknowledgment of violence and injustice—an admission to the effect that we are all indeed *ladrones*, thieves—and thus intent on destroying all myths of innocence by way of pointed recalling and constant reminding.

Second, such a reading is from an exile perspective insofar as it resists any type of spiritualization of the Bible in implicit support of the present order. It does not accept the presumably apolitical, but in fact highly political view, of a salvation that is otherworldly, a reign of God that is in the future, and a God who is interested in souls rather than bodies, in life after death rather than in the affairs of this world. It argues instead for a salvation that is highly social and political, a reign of God that is already at work in the world, and a God who demands justice and peace in all human dealings. Such a reading proceeds from a people who see the present order in terms of discrimination and marginalization and who struggle for a radically different order in the light of God's reign.

Finally, such a reading is naive insofar as it resists all sophisticated claims to objectivity vis-à-vis the Bible. It rejects the traditional academic claims to detachment and universality in interpretation, emphasizing instead, openly and explicitly, the perspectival nature of all readings (including its own) as well as its preference for a typological reading of the Bible as a text addressed to the people of God in their historical pilgrimage. As such, it is a reading that takes the Bible into its own hands and away from those in control of the present order, reading it from its own perspective rather than from the perspective of the powerful.

For González this reading "in Spanish" demands a specific reading "grammar" or strategy, consisting of four cardinal principles or rules.[23] First, given the highly political and social character of the texts, the reading must focus on the central question of power and powerlessness in the Bible. Second, given the largely communal orientation of the texts, as meant to be read in public rather than in private, the reading must see the Bible as addressing the community of faith. Third, given the principle of availability to "children" inherent in the texts, the reading must be particularly attuned to what "the children"—the poor and the simple—find in the Bible. Fourth, given the widespread use of the vocative in the texts, the reading must not only engage in interpreting the text but must also let itself be interpreted by the text, again with a vision of the Bible as addressing the people of God in their historical pilgrimage. In the end, González sees this reading of the Bible "in Spanish" as applicable to the entire theological tradition of the church, becoming thereby the fundamental reading strategy of *mañana* theology.

For *mañana* theology, as for barrio theology, it is the whole of the Bible that is central and authoritative. The message of both Old and New Testaments is one of liberation: God is fully at work in the social and political arenas of the world, demanding justice and peace in all human dealings. This message, however, is neither innocent nor idealized, but rather full of skeletons and failures from beginning to end: God remains fully at work in and through such a noninnocent and concrete history. The Bible is thus both liberating and noninnocent.[24] Such a message of

23. See, e.g., Justo L. González, "Pluralismo, justicia y misión: un estudio bíblico sobre Hechos 6:1-7," *Apuntes* 10 (1990): 3–8. See also González's *Faith and Wealth: A History of Early Christian Ideas on the Origin, Significance, and Use of Money* (San Francisco: Harper & Row, 1990).

24. González places (*Mañana*, 75–82) enormous emphasis on the importance and role of the Old Testament: just as the Old Testament is interpreted through the eyes of the New Testament, so must the New Testament be interpreted through the eyes of the Old Testament. Such emphasis emerges

liberation demands a specific way of reading, a reading from the perspective of exile. As a result, a basic correspondence is posited between the people of God in the Bible and Hispanic Americans: a people "in exile," alien and powerless, called to new life by God and thus in search of liberation; a people painfully aware of its history and identity, its beginnings in violence and injustice, resisting all attempts at an innocent idealization of history and serving as a sharp and constant reminder of the fact that in the end we are all *ladrones*.

For *mañana* theology, therefore, the situation and liberation of Hispanic Americans are anticipated in the life and calling of the people of God in the Bible: despite their own noninnocent history and identity, their many failures and skeletons, God calls them to liberation, to peace and justice, social change, and transformation in the world. As one of the many silent and marginalized peoples in the world, Hispanic Americans are also called to work toward a new *mañana* in the context of the new reformation unleashed in the church, a reformation ultimately described by González as far more substantial and profound than that of the sixteenth century.

A Hermeneutics of Liberation

As mentioned earlier in this study, the theological visions of these four Hispanic American theologians reveal a clear option for the optic and methodology of liberation theology; as such, they also reveal a corresponding preference for a hermeneutics of liberation in their approach to and reading of the Bible. In fact, these four visions represent—following the recent typology adopted by Christopher Rowland and Mark Corner in their

---

out of the deep suspicion that many are content to ignore or bypass the Old Testament in favor of the New, given the fact that the latter is much more susceptible to a spiritualized reading. As the writings of a nascent community, he explains, the New Testament's emphasis on peace and justice is not as explicit or as pervasive as the Old Testament's; this is why any marginalization of the latter must be resisted.

study of liberation hermeneutics—examples of a "correspondence in relationships," with a formal analogy drawn between the relationship of the Bible to its social context, howsoever conceived, and the relationship of the contemporary Christian community to its own social context.[25] Within this fundamental correspondence posited between Hispanic Americans and the Bible, one finds a number of different foci and emphases.

(1) From the point of view of perceived affinity with the text, of access on the part of present-day readers to texts coming from a very different culture and time period, one can see both direct identification and cautious distance. All three male theologians (Recinos, Elizondo, González) posit immediate identification (though they also grant the need to interpret the text in its own context—a position whose precise methodology remains, however, largely undeveloped): the life and struggles of the Hispanic American community, howsoever defined, have been anticipated in the life and struggles of the people of God in the Bible. The Bible is in and of itself liberating, and Hispanic Americans can readily identify with its message. Isasi-Díaz, as a female theologian, argues for a careful and discerning distance: the life and struggles of Hispanic American women have indeed been anticipated in the life and struggles of the biblical women; however, the Bible itself can be both liberating and oppressive for women, and thus, with regard to biblical interpretation, women must be constantly on their guard. The degree of affinity shows a clear gender-related dimension, with suspicion very much at work on the part of Isasi-Díaz.

(2) The view of the Bible as a liberating text involves two different theoretical positions: the concept of a canon within the

25. Christopher Rowland and Mark Corner, *Liberating Exegesis: The Challenge of Liberation Theology to Biblical Studies* (Louisville: John Knox/Westminster Press, 1989), 35–85. This typology is borrowed from the work of Clodovis Boff in *Theology and Praxis: Epistemological Foundations* (Maryknoll, N.Y.: Orbis Books, 1977).

canon and the notion of a unified and consistent text. The concept of the canon within the canon, used by both Isasi-Díaz and Elizondo, offers two variations. For Isasi-Díaz, it is the experience of Hispanic American women that is normative and authoritative, on the basis of which biblical texts are judged to be either liberating or oppressive for women. For Elizondo, it is a specific tradition within the Bible that becomes normative and authoritative—the life of the historical Jesus as recounted by the Synoptic Gospels.

The notion of a unified and consistent text, employed by both Recinos and González, presents two variations as well. For Recinos, the whole of the Bible is normative and authoritative: the tradition of liberation extends from beginning to end, from the early law codes of the Pentateuch to the writings of the early church. For González, the Bible as a whole is again normative and authoritative, but also noninnocent: the tradition of liberation unfolds in quite unlikely venues and with repeated failings from beginning to end. The locus of liberation varies, therefore, from the local (Isasi-Díaz, Elizondo) to the universal (Recinos, González), from the internal, both straightforward (Recinos, Elizondo) and complex (González), to the external (Isasi-Díaz). While the former variation reveals a certain church-related dimension, with Roman Catholics favoring the local and Protestants on the side of the universal, the latter variation again shows a clear gender-related element, with the male theologians on the side of the internal and the woman theologian favoring the external.

(3) For all four theologians, the entrée to the liberating power of the Bible lies in an experience of marginalization and oppression. Although their descriptions of such an experience share many points (social, economic, political, cultural) in common, particular emphases do emerge: (1) gender (Isasi-Díaz)—marginalization defined from the point of view of Hispanic American women, with a combined emphasis on sexism and racism; (2) socioeconomic oppression (Recinos)—marginalization in

terms of the desperate socioeconomic conditions of the barrio; (3) sociocultural rejection (Elizondo)—marginalization from the point of view of *mestizaje*, of racial and cultural mixture and impurity; and (4) sociohistorical situation (González)—marginalization in terms of exile and alienation. Consequently, the dominant message of liberation of the Bible can be readily summarized as follows in each case: the *mujerista* God of peace and justice, the God of the popular religiosity of Hispanic American women (Isasi-Díaz); the God of the barrio, the God of the poor and the oppressed (Recinos); the God of Jesus, the mestizo from Galilee, the message of the new universalism (Elizondo); and the noninnocent God of *mañana*, the God of exile, of the alien and the powerless (González).

(4) Such an entrée to the liberating power of the Bible calls for a specific way of reading the Bible, a reading of resistance characterized as not only correct but also biblical and contrasted with other readings coming from a perspective of power and privilege. Specifically, these theologians call for an experiential reading in accord with the core values of popular religiosity among Hispanic American women, vis-à-vis the interpretive lens of a patriarchal church (Isasi-Díaz); a prophetic reading from the perspective of the oppressed that reappropriates the basic story of the Bible, vis-à-vis a royal reading from the position of imperial authority that obfuscates and distorts this basic story (Recinos); a borderland reading faithful to the word of the gospel, to the message of universal inclusion, vis-à-vis an establishment reading of division and exclusion (Elizondo); a reading in the vernacular, "in Spanish," with a focus on issues of power and powerlessness, vis-à-vis all innocent, spiritualized, and sophisticated readings (González).

(5) Finally, such readings of the Bible are highly utopian and hence subversive, calling into question the present order of violence, injustice, and inequality in the world in the light of a new world already at work, based on equality, justice, and peace. In all four cases, therefore, the eschatological dimension of the

Bible is sharply highlighted: a vision of a world grounded in peace and love, where women suffer no longer from sexism and racism (Isasi-Díaz); a vision of a world based on justice and equality, where the ravaged regain a sense of human dignity (Recinos); a vision of a world based on racial and cultural inclusion, where an expanding global *mestizaje* leads to a celebration of diversity and new life for humanity (Elizondo); a vision of a world grounded in the values of the new reformation, where social transformation, radical ecumenism, and the active voice of all peoples usher in the era of a radically different *mañana* (González).

In conclusion, these readings of liberation emerging from the distinct social context and perspective of Hispanic Americans see the Bible as both an effective weapon in the struggle against marginalization and discrimination and a faithful ally in the struggle for liberation. The God of the Bible is not at all foreign or remote, but a God who works with and for Hispanic Americans. The people of God in the Bible are not at all temporally or culturally distant, but emerge as fellow sufferers, fellow pilgrims or sojourners, fellow visionaries. If read correctly, the Bible grants dignity, power, and direction; it changes and transforms; it leads out of oppression to liberation. Such open and explicit readings breathe and inspire liberation.

At the same time, such readings need to become even more self-conscious and self-critical, in line with the fundamental and ongoing task of self-criticism in liberation theology. In this regard, *mujerista* theology, as is generally the case with feminist theory and criticism, is already a step ahead. These fundamental issues of affinity with the text, locus of liberation, entrée to the text, proper and improper readings, and utopian visions need to be addressed head-on, not only in terms of biblical criticism but also in terms of both social and literary criticism, and in full dialogue with contemporary theology and biblical hermeneutics. In the end, I believe that such analysis and dialogue will gain for us, as Hispanic Americans, many more weapons and many more allies in the pursuit of our manifest destiny.

3

Rediscovering Praxis:
The Significance of U.S. Hispanic Experience for Theological Method

Roberto S. Goizueta

As U.S. Hispanic theologians attempt to develop a theological reflection born out of the historical experience of our communities, we are confronted with the question, What are we doing when we ground our reflection in that experience? Implicit in the question of theological context, or sources, is the question of theological method: What is the relationship between the *locus theologicus* (the context of theological reflection) and the theological enterprise itself? Insofar as U.S. Hispanic theologians seek to articulate a *teología de conjunto*, the question of methodology is fundamental and, thus, must be addressed explicitly if we are to be faithful to our explicit intent. At its core, the methodological question is that of the relationship between praxis and theory. This question has been particularly central to the development of liberation theologies insofar as these have sought to affirm the foundational significance of praxis over against modern Western conceptualism and rationalism.[1]

Informed by the insights of Latin American liberation theologians, U.S. Hispanic theologians likewise affirm the foundational import of praxis. At the same time, however, we recognize that any uncritical assimilation of Latin American liberation theology would represent a betrayal of the very methodology that we affirm; the uncritical assimilation of any theological model would represent a failure to ground our reflection in the experience of our own communities, the communities of Hispanics living in the United States. As U.S. Hispanic *theologians*, we seek to learn from other theologians; as *U.S. Hispanic* theologians, we seek to redefine the theological task by locating it within the praxis of U.S. Hispanic communities—thereby redefining praxis itself as the foundation of theology.

It is equally clear that an uncritical repudiation of modern Western theological movements would, likewise, represent an infidelity to the praxis of our communities inasmuch as, for better or worse, these communities participate in modern Western history—even if principally as the bearers of its dehumanizing consequences. Any uncritical rejection of Western theology would imply a concomitant rejection of our historical praxis as *U.S. Hispanics*. The task confronting us, therefore, is one of neither assimilation nor repudiation; it is, rather, a task of critical appropriation. Such a task requires that we approach and critique

---

1. Many of the questions raised and ideas articulated in this article were initially set forth in a paper I presented at the 1991 annual convention of the Catholic Theological Society of America, held in Atlanta "Theology as Intellectually Vital Inquiry: The Challenge of/to U.S. Hispanic Theologians," appears in the *Proceedings of Catholic Theological Society of America* 46 (1991): 58–69. These represent, in turn, a development of the reflections on theory and praxis proffered in my 1990 presidential address to the Academy of Catholic Hispanic Theologians of the United States, and in my essay "U.S. Hispanic Theology and the Challenge of Pluralism," *Frontiers of a United States Hispanic Theology*, ed. Allan Figueroa Deck (Maryknoll, N.Y.: Orbis Books, 1992).

traditional theological sources and methods, whether European or Latin American, from the perspective of U.S. Hispanics in order to be able to articulate the significance of that perspective for the life of our communities, the church, and society.

To suggest possible ways in which the U.S. Hispanic experience might contribute to an understanding of praxis and, hence, theological method, we will (1) examine critically, if briefly, the modern Western notion of praxis; (2) trace the emergence of that notion by examining the interpretations of praxis that have exerted the greatest influence on Western thought; (3) examine the notion and role of praxis as reinterpreted within Latin American liberation theology; (4) suggest how U.S. Hispanic theologians might learn from (1), (2), and (3) while at the same time moving beyond these, thereby contributing to the theological task of the church and the academy; and, finally, (5) explore how the U.S. Hispanic experience might contribute to an understanding of the relationship between praxis and theory.

The History of Praxis

Aristotle, Marx, and Liberation Theology

That the notion of praxis has a long history is a fact that has all too often been ignored in the midst of contemporary debate about the primacy of praxis in the theological enterprise and, indeed, in the everyday life of the Christian. If U.S. Hispanic theologians are to make a significant contribution to this debate about the nature of not only Christian theology, but also Christian faith (for example, orthodoxy vis-à-vis orthopraxis), a critical retrieval of that history will facilitate such a contribution by revealing the lacunae and distortions in the contemporary debate and suggesting ways in which we might help address these. With its own roots in communities still influenced by premodern cultures, our theological reflection may then be able to effect a critical retrieval of premodern Western notions of praxis, which have been distorted by modern Cartesian epistemologies. At the same time, as rooted in premodern cultures marginalized by Western imperialism, the historical praxis of our communities would provide a critique of premodern Western notions of praxis that do not attend to the demands of social transformation.

By virtue of its manifold meanings and etymological history, the term *praxis* is much more multivalent than is indicated by its usage in many contemporary contexts, where the word is often employed as a synonym for "practice." Indeed, as Hans-Georg Gadamer, Jürgen Habermas, Richard Bernstein, Matthew Lamb, and others have observed, the modern notion of practice is itself reductionist, and hence distorted.[2] Gadamer, for example, writes that "the concept of '*praxis*' which has developed in the last two centuries is an awful deformation of what practice really is. In all the debates of the last century practice was understood as application of science to technical tasks. . . . It degrades practical reason to technical control."[3] Lamb contends that, in the context of the natural sciences' epistemological hegemony, "modern notions of praxis all tend either to connote or explicitly invoke *movement*. . . . In such a context the call to praxis could mean no more than a call to practicality . . . for if all human activity is basically just another species of movement, then being practical means learning the skills and techniques of control."[4] Among the key historical factors influencing this process of distortion has been the intellectual

2. See, e.g., Hans-Georg Gadamer, "Hermeneutics and Social Science," *Cultural Hermeneutics* 2 (1975): 307-16; Jürgen Habermas, *The Theory of Communicative Action* (Boston: Beacon Press, 1984); Richard Bernstein, *Beyond Objectivism and Relativism: Science, Hermeneutics, and Praxis* (Philadelphia: University of Pennsylvania Press, 1985); Matthew Lamb, *Solidarity with Victims* (New York: Crossroad, 1982); and Lamb, "Praxis," in *The New Dictionary of Theology*, ed. Joseph Komonchak, Mary Collins, and Dermot Lane (Wilmington, Del.: Michael Glazier, 1988), 784–87.
3. Gadamer, "Hermeneutics and Social Science," 312.
4. Lamb, "Praxis," 785.

hegemony exercised by Cartesian and scientific epistemological paradigms. If praxis is but the action of a Cartesian ego upon an external object (for example, another human "individual"), an action that implies movement, praxis is reduced to mere technique; that is, praxis is defined as the subject's control and manipulation of the external object in order to achieve some predetermined end.[5]

Yet the reduction of praxis to practice remains incomplete, and thus ambiguous, insofar as the effects of praxis are understood to be not only external, with respect to the object being controlled or manipulated, but also internal, with respect to the subject. That is, the subject's praxis in the world is seen as contributing to the empowerment and liberation of the subject. The modern notion of praxis suffers from this ambiguity between the external, or technical, and internal, or humanistic, ends of human praxis.[6]

The unintended, destructive consequences of so many modern ideologies derive precisely from a failure to attend adequately to this ambiguity. Lured by the humanistic claims of praxis as an instrument for empowerment and liberation, Marxists and others have not been sufficently attentive to the ambiguities present in this instrumentalization of praxis—however noble the ends that are sought. Whatever our ends, the instruments we employ (in this case, human praxis and, hence, human beings) always remain ambiguous because all instruments, insofar as they utilize the external environment in order to achieve those ends, necessarily involve manipulation and control—that is, coercion. To ignore this ambiguity is to undermine precisely those ends that we seek.

The identification of praxis with practice, and practice with technique, reveals a contradiction internal to modern praxis-based theories of change, for these predicate the achievement

5. Ibid.
6. Ibid., 785–86; Goizueta, "Theology as Intellectually Vital Inquiry."

of human freedom on the application of techniques and strategies to the social world, which, of course, includes human beings. The human person becomes an object to be utilized, through praxis, to achieve a higher end, even if that end is the supposed transformation or liberation of the person himself or herself. Moreover, even when the person is perceived as his or her own agent of liberation, praxis becomes the means whereby the concrete, historical person in the present recreates himself or herself (that is, "works upon" himself or herself as if upon an object), thereby achieving self-esteem, self-worth, and liberation. Concrete persons then derive their value from their ability to turn themselves into instruments of their own liberation, or to make the present (historical praxis) an instrument for creating the future; this implies a process of self-objectification. While the process of human growth and development is always important, one must not lose sight of the tendency therein to devalue present, concrete life, however ugly, by perceiving it as simply the raw material to be used in the creation of the future "new person." To the extent that the present is thus instrumentalized, concrete, historical praxis is subordinated to a conceptual reality, whether "the Future" or "the New Person." Human life, or praxis, is sacrificed to the concept.

Consequently, the modern tendency to identify praxis with technique has led to an identification of knowledge itself—*all* knowledge—with the conceptual, empiricist, and technological; in other words, the reduction of knowledge to what can be observed, measured, quantified, and thus brought under our control. Any aspect of life that is not thus observable, measurable, or quantifiable is deemed impractical and thus irrelevant and meaningless. Value is identified with practicality, and practicality is, in turn, defined in terms of quantifiable criteria.[7]

The danger of falling prey to such reductionism can only be averted if the external, objectivizing, and transformative ends

7. See Lamb, "Praxis."

of praxis are grounded in concrete human praxis *as an end in itself.* To correct the modern distortions, numerous scholars have essayed a critical retrieval of the premodern, Aristotelian notion of praxis.[8] Aristotle uses the term *praxis* to denote all human activity whose end is internal rather than external to itself. He thus distinguishes praxis, activity that is an end in itself, from *poiesis,* activity that seeks some end external to the performance itself, and distinguishes both of these from *theoria.* The paradigmatic examples of praxis are political activity and moral conduct. The difference between praxis and poiesis may be rendered as that between doing and making, where the former is its own reward while the latter seeks its reward in the results of the performance; the end of praxis is the praxis itself, whereas the end of poiesis is the result left over after one has completed the task.[9] Given this distinction, the fundamental form of praxis is nothing other than life, or living, itself; in the *Politics,* Aristotle avers that "life is action [praxis] and not production [poiesis]."[10]

8. In the North American context, see, e.g., Alasdair MacIntyre, *After Virtue: A Study in Moral Theory* (Notre Dame, Ind.: University of Notre Dame Press, 1981) and *Whose Justice? Which Rationality?* (Notre Dame, Ind.: University of Notre Dame Press, 1988).

9. Nicholas Lobkowicz, *Theory and Practice: History of a Concept from Aristotle to Marx* (Notre Dame, Ind.: University of Notre Dame Press, 1967), 9-11. Lobkowicz illustrates this difference by comparing the activity of playing a flute (praxis) with that of building a house (poiesis): "An activity such as building a house would never be considered satisfactory if it did not stop, that is, resulted in a house built and finished. As opposed to this, . . . playing the flute obviously has achieved its end a long time before it stops. In fact, once it has stopped, it is no longer of any value—precisely because it does not aim at a result beyond the mere 'doing' of it" (p. 10). Lamb provides a further illustration: "What Aristotle was on to is the difference drawn, for example, between a house and a home. Productive techniques are needed to make a house. But a home is a doing, a performing, a praxis which is a good in itself when it is achieved; and the achievement of the happiness which is a family home requires much more than management techniques: a home requires virtuous parents and children" ("Praxis," 786).

10. Aristotle, *Politics* I, 4, 1254; see also his *Nicomachean Ethics*, VI, 4, 1140.

ROBERTO S. GOIZUETA

The distinction becomes blurred, however, in the (much later) Marxian notion of praxis. If Aristotle identifies human life with praxis, inasmuch as life is always an end in itself, Marx identifies human life with productive labor, for it is through labor that we actualize, or "produce," ourselves as persons: "Conscious life-activity directly distinguishes man from animal life-activity. . . . In creating an objective world by his practical activity, in working-up inorganic nature, man proves himself a conscious species being."[11] What defines human praxis, or "conscious life-activity," is its productive capacity; the person becomes a person (praxis) by his or her ability to "create an objective world" (poiesis).[12] Praxis is thus reduced to poiesis. Indeed, Marx's fundamental criticism of capitalism is precisely that, in capitalism, productive labor is seen as merely a means to an end (survival), whereas, for Marx, human productive labor (poiesis) is "life-activity" itself (praxis)—that which defines the human as human. For Marx, praxis is predicated on, and thus subordinated to, poiesis. This anthropology underlies Marx's historical materialism: the mode of production is the engine of history.[13]

Alienation results when productive labor, through which humankind produces itself, is no longer viewed as an end in itself, but as merely a means to an external end (which, of course, is exactly how Aristotle saw it). Our labor is what distinguishes us from animals; it is in our work that we should experience

11. Karl Marx, "Economic and Philosophic Manuscripts of 1844," in *The Marx-Engels Reader*, ed. Robert C. Tucker (New York: W. W. Norton & Co., 1978), 76.
12. Ibid., 73–76.
13. It is only fair to note that, while so-called orthodox Marxism came to interpret Marx in this reductionist manner, there are elements of Marx's thought, especially in his early writings, that would support arguments against such a reductionist interpretation. This fact is alluded to, for example, by Clodovis Boff in his discussion of Marx's notion of praxis in *Theology and Praxis,* 331.

ourselves as most human. The problem with capitalism, argues Marx, is that it fails to account for the fact that human productive activity is not only a means to life but is, in fact, the very meaning of life itself—at least human life.[14]

This close identification of human activity with productive activity leads to a blurring of the distinction between praxis and poiesis. What Aristotle had conceived as but a means becomes, with Marx and, especially, so-called orthodox Marxism, an end in itself—indeed, the privileged characteristic that defines our existence as human. If part of the Marxian legacy is the important recognition of productive activity as constitutive of the human, an equally significant part of that legacy is the attenuation of the Aristotelian distinction between human activity and productive activity. The historical transition from the premodern, Aristotelian notion of praxis to the modern, Marxian notion of praxis is outlined by Clodovis Boff in his book *Theology and Praxis*:

> Aristotle sees a neat distinction between *praxis* and *poiesis*. Praxis is a form of activity characterized by its immanence: its development is its own end. . . . As for the second form of activity (*operatio-poiesis*) . . . we have a *transitive* activity: its finality is something other than itself. . . . In current usage, "praxis" means both types of activity discerned by Aristotle. . . . Primarily owing to the ideological and historical pressure of Marxism, praxis is no longer understood as its own end, *Selbstzweck*, self-finalized activity—but on the contrary, as the production of an external result. Praxis is action resulting in an effect of transformation. . . . The semantic reverse of the term is total, then.[15]

What Marx—like all modernity—failed to appreciate is the ambiguity inherent in any notion of human praxis that defines it in terms of production, even if what is being produced is "the just person" or "the just society." Production necessarily involves manipulation and coercion, and these are, at best, ambiguous instruments of liberation. Recent centuries are strewn

14. Marx, "Economic and Philosophic Manuscripts."
15. Boff, *Theology and Praxis*, 331.

with the victims of nations and leaders who, inspired by a Rousseauian magnanimity, have insisted on forcing people to be free. Marx's antidote to the instrumentalization of human life that he identifies with modern capitalist society is thus . . . instrumentalization, albeit toward an ostensibly more noble end. If, in capitalism, the life of the worker becomes an object to be manipulated in the service of the commodity, in Marxism the life of the worker becomes an object to be manipulated—even if by the worker himself or herself—in the service of the future "New Person": "his own life is an object for him."[16] What neither ideology appreciates is that to make life an object to be worked upon is to instrumentalize life and thus, inevitably, to kill life.

Any notion of praxis that subordinates the concrete present to the hoped-for future undermines not only the present but that future as well. The fall of the Berlin Wall in the socialist East and the environmental crisis, urban crisis, drug epidemic, and moral breakdown in the capitalist West serve as reminders that the attempt to make the concrete present the instrument for achieving a hoped-for idyllic future will always be self-defeating.

Latin American liberation theology emerges from the underside of modernity to critique its dark side, the consequences of which the people of Latin America continue to bear. At the same time, liberation theology inherits some of the ambiguities latent in modern views of praxis, particularly insofar as liberation theologians are influenced by the Marxian notion of praxis. In the formative writings of the liberation theology movement, the notion of praxis is sometimes given several meanings, often overlapping ones. In its broadest sense, the term refers to historical praxis, which Gustavo Gutiérrez defines as simply a person's "active presence in history."[17] A second, more specific

16. Marx, "Economic and Philosophic Manuscripts," 76.
17. Gustavo Gutiérrez, *A Theology of Liberation,* rev. ed. (Maryknoll, N.Y.: Orbis Books, 1988), 6.

meaning is that of Christian praxis, the specifically Christian way of being actively present in history through commitment and prayer, action and contemplation.[18] In its third, most particular sense, the term specifies, with greater concreteness, just what Christian commitment and prayer entail, namely, liberating praxis: "The praxis on which liberation theology reflects is a praxis of solidarity in the interests of liberation and is inspired by the gospel. . . . Consequently, a praxis motivated by evangelical values embraces to some extent every effort to bring about authentic fellowship and authentic justice. . . . This liberating praxis endeavors to transform history in the light of the reign of God."[19]

The significance of this methodological emphasis on transformation as foundational for theology cannot be overestimated; it is perhaps the most important contribution of liberation theology. Yet the term liberating praxis itself contains an ambiguity: Is liberation a concomitant or a goal of praxis? If the former is true, then praxis is its own end: one becomes free in the very act or process of transforming history. If the latter is true, then the end of praxis is external to the praxis itself: one becomes free *after* one has transformed history. The first understanding of praxis tends toward a more Aristotelian view, whereas the latter tends toward a more Marxian view.[20] Both of these views can be found in the writings of liberation theologians and in the liberation theology movement itself: (the former in the emphasis on the self-empowerment of the poor as the subjects of social transformation, and the latter in the very call for social transformation.) Yet the relationship between these two dimensions

18. Ibid., xxxiv, 6.
19. Ibid., xxx.
20. I do not mean to set up a simple dichotomy here, but merely to suggest different tendencies.

of praxis—praxis as *intrinsically* liberative and praxis as yielding a liberative *result*—needs to be addressed more systematically.[21]

Contributions of U.S. Hispanic Experience

As critical reflection on praxis, the theology being developed by U.S. Hispanics is informed by the methodology of Latin American liberation theology. At the same time, however, a genuine fidelity to this methodology will imply that the content of our theological reflection will differ from its Latin American counterpart; that is, because the historical praxis of U.S. Hispanic communities is different (even if similar in important ways), that praxis will yield a different understanding of the community's faith. More specifically, the concrete historicity of U.S. Hispanic communities will furnish new insights into the very meaning of historicity, or praxis, itself.

These new insights (or, perhaps more correctly, new emphases) which, while present in some liberation theology, have taken on a new centrality in the theological reflection of U.S. Hispanics, offer us a way of addressing the ambiguities and contradictions latent in the modern notions of praxis to which we, as theologians, are heirs. That U.S. Hispanic praxis offers us resources for addressing those ambiguities is evident, above all, in the centrality accorded popular religiosity as a principal expression of the historical praxis of our communities.[22] By

21. One of the most brilliant attempts to perform such a correlation is Boff's *Theology and Praxis*.

22. A number of Latin American liberation theologians have also paid special attention to popular religiosity: see, e.g., Juan Carlos Scannone, "Enfoques teológico-pastorales latinoamericanos de la religiosidad popular," *Stromata* 40 (1985): 33–47; Segundo Galilea, *Religiosidad popular y pastoral* (Madrid: Ediciones Cristiandad, 1979), and "The Theology of Liberation and the Place of Folk Religion," in *What Is Religion? An Inquiry for Christian Theology* (Edinburgh: T. & T. Clark, 1980), 40–45. Yet popular religiosity has not generally attained the methodological significance in the Latin American liberation theology movement as a whole that it has among U.S. Hispanic

emphasizing the popular religious character of historical praxis, U.S. Hispanic theologians are emphasizing the inherently communal and aesthetic character of praxis, without, on the other hand, depreciating its transformative character.

Virgilio Elizondo, Orlando Espín, Sixto García, and other U.S. Hispanic theologians have observed that the popular religiosity of U.S. Hispanics is, for us, a principal way of being in the world.[23] Even though not all Latinos and Latinas are regularly involved in the performance of religious devotions, or are even believers, all share a common *manera de ser*, or way of being, which both presupposes and affirms relationality and sacramentality as fundamental realities definitive of human praxis. This way of being then finds ritual expression not only in popular religious devotions but in everyday language as well. Espín and García refer, for instance, to the popular religious character of wisdom phrases, such as *si Dios quiere* ("if God wills it"), *¡Jesús, María y José!*, or *Dios sabe lo que hace* ("God knows what God is doing").[24] These and other such exclamatory and aphoristic sayings are an inextricable part of U.S. Hispanic culture in a way that similar sayings in Anglo American culture

---

theologians—at least thus far. A major reason for this difference in emphasis is the centrality of cultural oppression to the experience of Hispanics living in an alien society; the salience of popular religious praxis as an expression of cultural identity is enhanced where the distinctiveness of that identity becomes more visible. While Latin Americans suffer from devastating forms of cultural oppression vis-à-vis the cultures of North America and Europe (often filtered through the cultures of local elites), the distinctiveness of Latin American culture naturally comes to the fore and becomes more visible when transplanted into the United States, thereby increasing the availability of cultural difference as an instrument of marginalization.

23. See, e.g., Elizondo, *Galilean Journey* and *The Future Is Mestizo;* Orlando O. Espín and Sixto J. García, eds. "Lilies of the Field: A Hispanic Theology of Providence and Human Responsibility," *Proceedings of the Catholic Theological Society of America* 44 (1989): 70–90; Orlando O. Espín, "Tradition and Popular Religion: An Understanding of the *Sensus Fidelium,*" in *Frontiers of U.S. Hispanic Theology;* Deck, *The Second Wave,* 113–19.

24. Espín and García, "Lilies of the Field," 76–77.

are not; indeed, such ritualistic invocations of the deity would often be deemed unseemly, if not blasphemous, by the dominant culture. In short, popular religiosity is but the expression, in symbol and ritual, of the historical praxis of our U.S. Hispanic communities.

What popular religiosity expresses, above all, is the communal and aesthetic character of praxis. In its most basic sense, popular religiosity is the affirmation of an essential social and cosmic solidarity as intrinsic and foundational to human praxis; conversely, injustice, alienation, and oppression are distortions of praxis. The fundamental goal of popular religiosity is the practical, performative, and participatory affirmation of community as the foundation of all human activity. That community includes not only our contemporaries but also past and future generations; it likewise includes God and the saints. The principal metaphor for this community is the family.[25]

The community implicit in praxis is not, however, the modern Western community, understood as a voluntary association of atomic individuals; rather it is an organic reality in which the relationship between persons is not only extrinsic but, at a more fundamental level, intrinsic as well. In and through praxis, the intrinsic unity of person, community, and God is affirmed. In the praxis of the modern Western subject, the subject has ontological priority, for he or she chooses community; in the praxis of U.S. Hispanics, community has ontological priority, for it gives birth to subjectivity. Virgilio Elizondo describes the difference between these two views of community:

> For our native forefathers, it was not the individuals who by coming together made up the community, but rather it was the community which had been developing since the Lord and Lady of creation allowed man and woman to descend unto earth through the many generations of their ancestors which actually brought the individual person into

25. Ibid., 78.

existence. . . . Thus it was the community which called forth the individuality of the person. The unique way in which the person embodied the ways and traditions of the group determined his/her individuality. It was the community which made the individual person: it accepted to make him/her at baptism, it called him/her into existence through the educational process of the group and sustained him/her in existence through the various closely-knit systems of inter-relationships not only with the various members of the clan, but also with all of nature and even with the astral world.[26]

The modern Western subject forges a self-identity by distancing himself or herself from community (for example, family) and tradition in order to achieve autonomy and independence; the U.S. Hispanic, on the other hand, derives his or her identity from that very community, which remains an important part of self-identity even if the person should physically leave the formative community.[27]

The essential goal of popular religious praxis is the affirmation and perpetuation of these ontological bonds. Popular religiosity represents the practical affirmation of the interpersonal bonds existing among persons, Christ, Mary, and the saints, all of whom are treated not as "powerful, sacred entities" but as "members of the family."[28] If popular religious praxis is perceived through Western, Enlightenment lenses as a superstitious attempt at spiritual manipulation, for U.S. Hispanics it is, at bottom, simply a practical or performative reaffirmation

26. Virgilio Elizondo, *La Morenita: Evangelizer of the Americas* (San Antonio: Mexican American Cultural Center, 1980), 8.

27. In *La Morenita*, Elizondo presents a comparison of the Greek notion of education, or *paideia*, and the notion of education prevalent in indigenous communities, where "the most important aspect of education was the integration of the individual, from the very beginning, into the life of the group which would always be a significant part. . . . It was the group, with its living tradition, which had originated with the gods before time existed and which, thus, 'created' the individual and kept him in existence" (p. 16). Indeed, the Spanish word for "to raise" (as in "to raise" children) is *criar*, which comes from the same root as *crear*, to create.

28. Espín and García, "Lilies of the Field," 78.

---

of the intrinsic value of these relationships. Elizondo describes
the organic cosmovision underlying the Mexican symbol of
Tonantzín, which eventually developed into the Christian symbol of Guadalupe: the cosmic force represented by Tonantzín
"acted as a sort of collective soul which thereby brought about
the intrinsic unity of everything which is. . . . *Nothing is un-
related*. . . . We do not find ourselves in the presence of 'large
chains of rationalizations,' but in a reciprocal and continuous
implication of the diverse aspects of a single totality."[29] Popular
religiosity, then, "is the way in which masses of the people
express their communion with the ultimate, and through this
communion find meaning and strength in their lives."[30] In other
words, the end of popular religiosity is this interpersonal relationship itself.

The possibility and, indeed, the obligation of social transformation arises out of this internal end of praxis. Insofar as
human praxis reveals the ontological priority of community as
intrinsic to historical praxis, it also implies an ethical-political
obligation to struggle against every obstacle to such community.[31] The demand for social transformation is not extrinsic to
personal praxis; that is, such a demand does not presuppose an
isolated subject who is confronted by community and society
with their ethical-political demands. On the contrary, those demands are intrinsic to praxis since they are already presupposed
in the very constitution of the person, who is always inherently
and unavoidably social by nature. The intrinsic communal character of praxis grounds and makes possible its extrinsic ethical-
political orientation.[32] To say that the marginalized (for example,

29. Elizondo, *La Morenita*, 23.
30. Ibid., 75.
31. Ibid., 8–9.
32. This fact is overlooked when popular religiosity, as a mediation of
historical praxis, is instrumentalized, or judged according to its usefulness for
social transformation. Since popular religiosity does not lead directly to social

U.S. Hispanics) have an epistemological privilege is to say that the experience of alienation, injustice, and oppression is the lens through which these are revealed as distortions of a fundamentally organic reality. The poor can continue to celebrate life in the midst of the struggle against death precisely because that struggle is what reveals the illusory nature of death's claims to ultimacy—in the same way as the passion and crucifixion of Jesus reveal the illusory nature of the principalities' and powers' claims to ultimacy.

From the perspective of the U.S. Hispanic experience praxis is revealed as not only inherently communal but also inherently celebratory, or aesthetic. The centrality of music, dance, and ritual in Hispanic life reveals the aesthetic sense underlying that life. Insofar as praxis is an affirmation of community, it is an affirmation of community as the highest form of beauty. Popular religiosity reveals praxis as communal, aesthetic performance.[33] Again, the fundamental end of praxis is not extrinsic but intrinsic, since that end is the practical, performative affirmation of the essential beauty of community in cosmos and history. Beauty is an end in itself; to instrumentalize beauty is to destroy it.

---

transformation, it is then deemed inadequate as a tool for social change. The fundamental mistake made here is that of using technological criteria as the basis for judging human praxis.

33. In their discussion of the centrality of aesthetics to Hispanic culture, Isasi-Díaz and Tarango describe how life is liturgized in Hispanic culture: *Hispanic Women*, 100–101. As an alternative to the Cartesian epistemological paradigm, the aesthetic paradigm has played an important role in the history of Latin American philosphy. See, especially, the works of José Vasconcelos, e.g., *Estética*, in *Obras completas*, III (México: Libreros Mexicanos Unidos, 1961), 1111–1711, and *El monismo estético* and *Filosofía estética*, in ibid., IV, 9–92 and 817–954, respectively. For an analysis of the aesthetic dimension of human praxis within the context of German critical theory, see Shierry M. Weber, "Aesthetic Experience and Self-Reflection as Emancipatory Processes: Two Complementary Aspects of Critical Theory," in *On Critical Theory*, ed. John O'Neill (New York: Seabury Press, 1976), 78–103.

Like the ontological priority of community, however, the ontological priority of beauty has important and necessary ethical-political implications, which are revealed by the experience of suffering. The experience and memories of suffering preclude a sentimentalized aesthetics. Sociohistorical nonidentity mediates aesthetic nonidentity; the historical praxis of the oppressed mediates aesthetic praxis. Consequently, the memories of suffering expressed in U.S. Hispanic popular religiosity—the memories of a vanquished people—prevent us from romanticizing popular religious devotions, music, and ritual, as so often occurs when these are portrayed in the communications media of the dominant culture.

Popular religiosity is an anamnestic performance, or praxis, that, in reenacting the suffering of our people, simultaneously reminds us that that suffering is not the last word. It is no coincidence that the Crucified Jesus and the Virgin Mary are so central to U.S. Hispanic popular religiosity. By identifying with the anguish of the Crucified, we recall the anguish of our people, which, like the cross, is the seedbed of our liberation. By identifying with Mary, especially in her various patronal manifestations, we likewise recall her special concern for the downtrodden, reflected in the fact that those whom she chooses as her messengers are usually poor people of indigenous, mestizo, or mulatto background. When we look at Mary, we see the visage of our people. According to Elizondo, "'La Virgen de Tepeyac' is the very core to understanding the struggle of the contemporary Mexican, born out of the violent intercourse of Spain and Mexico—of the Old World father and the New World mother. Each generation of Mexicans has been able to see mirrored in the *tilma* [cloak] the reflections of its sufferings, struggles, life, and ideals."[34] Describing the cultural and religious syncretism that gives rise to the Cuban symbol of *Nuestra Señora*

34. Elizondo, *La Morenita*, 69.

de la Caridad del Cobre (Our Lady of Charity), José Juan Arrom writes that "in this synthesis of creeds and hopes beats the soul of the Cuban people."[35] Like Mary, we suffer at the foot of the cross and, like Mary, are emboldened by the news that "he is risen." Our anamnestic solidarity with Jesus and Mary is thus, at the same time, the source of the hope that compels us to struggle for justice.

Insofar as popular religiosity has a subversive character, then, such an orientation toward the subversion of social forces of oppression is derived from its character as communal and aesthetic praxis. By affirming community in the face of oppression, and the beauty of creation in the face of de-creation and destruction, popular religious praxis becomes, indirectly, a crucial source of empowerment and liberation. When popular religiosity is used as a tool of liberation, the praxis of our communities is instrumentalized—that is, *we* are instrumentalized and, indeed, encouraged to view ourselves as instruments of some grand historical design. Such a distortion can only lead to new forms of oppression as the vibrant life (praxis) of our people, expressed in our popular religiosity, is no longer enjoyed as an end in itself, which engenders self-esteem and hope; that life becomes, instead, an object to be manipulated in the service of a presumably higher end. Concrete life is sacrificed to a conceptual future.

The Rationality of U.S. Hispanic Praxis

To assert that the extrinsic ends of praxis must be grounded in its intrinsic ends is not to imply, however, that reflection is to be depreciated. Indeed, the fact that praxis is always *historical* praxis implies that reflection is itself intrinsic to praxis as surely as the mind is intrinsic to the person. As Ada María Isasi-Díaz

---

35. José Juan Arrom, *Certidumbre de América: Estudios de letras, folklore y cultura* (Madrid: Editorial Gredos, 1971), 214 (my translation).

and Yolanda Tarango point out, "praxis is not reflection that follows action or is 'at the service of action.' Both action and reflection become inseparable moments in praxis. . . . To bring reflection to bear upon action—that is praxis."[36]

One of the most pernicious legacies of Cartesian and Kantian epistemological paradigms has been the tendency to divorce praxis from theory. Theory is then perceived to be inherently impractical, and praxis is perceived to be inherently irrational. Within the modern paradigm, the only solution to such a dichotomy—the only way to make theory "practical" and praxis "rational"—is to reduce praxis to an instrument of theory. Among the consequences of this radical split has been the dichotomy between the natural sciences, characterized as empiricist, positivist, and instrumentalist, and the human sciences, characterized as humanistic. Moreover, this dichotomy internally divides the various disciplines themselves, so that, for instance, empiricist and functionalist schools in the social sciences are perennially at odds with schools of critical theory. In the former, only theory that is practical, measurable, and verifiable with scientific certainty will be considered genuine knowledge; all other theory—including the insights of poets, philosophers, and theologians—is dismissed as mere speculation. Likewise, only praxis that is practical, measurable, and scientifically verifiable is to be taken seriously; all other praxis, such as popular religiosity, is to be discounted as irrelevant.[37]

The internal logic of this modern dilemma must ultimately lead, however, to the rejection of *all* knowledge (to wit, postmodern deconstruction), since even technical knowledge is, after all, useless until it is actually put into practice; in itself, all knowledge is useless. The logical outcome of the modern dichotomy is thus a radical suspicion of all theory, whether in the

36. Isasi-Díaz and Tarango, *Hispanic Women*, 1.
37. Lamb, "Praxis."

natural sciences or the humanistic sciences, since all theory is seen as, by its very nature, removed from reality. The postmodern repudiation of reason is but the logical outcome of the modern worship of reason.[38]

As U.S. Hispanic theologians attempt to articulate the significance of praxis for our theological reflection, we find ourselves caught in the middle of this epistemological crisis. Committed to doing theology from within a self-conscious solidarity with the historical struggles of U.S. Hispanic communities, ours is a praxis-based theology. We reject conceptualist theologies that remain inattentive to their historicity. Yet given the contemporary intellectual climate, where the only alternatives appear to be either the enshrinement of conceptualist, instrumentalist reason (modernity) or the repudiation of all reason (poststructuralist postmodernism), we should not allow ourselves to accept these as the only viable alternatives.[39] As U.S. Hispanics confront the modern rationalist ideologies that have repressed and suppressed our historical praxis for so long, the temptation will be to identify with that praxis over against the rationalism that has for so long served the interests of the dominant society. The danger is that, in an intellectual and social ambience where rationalism is identified not with an ahistorical, conceptualist reason, but with reason itself, we will allow our rejection of rationalism to become a rejection of reason and the intellectual enterprise as such. Our commitment to praxis would then no longer ground our theological reflection, but would instead replace theological reflection. Nothing could undermine

38. The modern Cartesian paradigm reduces reason to theory, and theory to concept, thereby paving the way for postmodernity, which accepts the basic dualistic presuppositions underlying the Cartesian paradigm, to reject not only conceptualism but reason itself.

39. On poststructuralist postmodernism, see Hal Foster, "(Post)Modern Polemics," *New German Critique* 33 (Fall 1984): 67–78; and Mark Kline Taylor, *Remembering Esperanza: A Cultural-Political Theology for North American Praxis* (Maryknoll, N.Y.: Orbis Books, 1990), 23–45.

the cause of U.S. Hispanics more than an uncritical (even if unwitting) assimilation of the modern Western epistemological dilemma.

If U.S. Hispanic praxis reveals the inherently communal and aesthetic character of praxis, this insight does not diminish the significance of the intellectual enterprise. On the contrary, as we uncover the foundational import of community and beauty, we likewise expand the scope of reason to include these: the recovery of community and beauty as intrinsic to human praxis is a supremely rational endeavor.[40] To ground theory in praxis is to opt for reason, though, of course, not the ahistorical, conceptualist, and instrumentalist reason of modernity. It is this latter that is revealed as utterly irrational in the face of the human and ecological carnage that modern ideologies have left in their wake.

For U.S. Hispanics to overlook the inherent rationality or reasonableness of communal and aesthetic praxis, and the consequent ethical-political exigencies, would be to fall prey to the very epistemological dichotomy that continues to legitimate the oppression of our communities. In the context of that dichotomy, Hispanic culture has been portrayed as a culture of the body, of feelings, of sensuality, and hence of praxis, in contrast to the dominant Anglo American culture, which is assumed to be a culture of the mind, of reason, of science, and hence of theory. Caught in this modern dichotomy, Hispanic culture is simultaneously idealized and marginalized: the same sense of community and beauty for which our culture is rightly admired becomes the justification for its denigration and marginalization,

---

40. The roots of community are not in feelings, but in ontology, in our very identity or nature as human beings and creatures, which includes but is not reducible to feelings; see my "Theology as Intellectually Vital Inquiry." Isasi-Díaz and Tarango warn against the dangers of sentimentalization; quoting Gloria Durka, they speak of aesthetics as "characterized by feeling *reasoned* and *feeling* reason"; *Hispanic Women*, 100.

since the commitment to community and beauty is perceived as irrational in a world dominated by individualist, rationalist, and scientific epistemological paradigms. The result is, at best, a patronizing condescension toward Latinos and Latinas. As Isasi-Díaz has pointed out, "this society deals with you [Hispanics] the way they do with a circus: they love our mariachis, salsa, *arroz con pollo, bacaladitos,* margaritas—we can really entertain them."[41]

Postmodern paradigms offer little more hope. Despite the understandable lure of postmodern retrievals of otherness, social situation, and aesthetics, postmodernism remains beholden to modern epistemological dualisms insofar as, in postmodernism, the retrieval of otherness, social situation, and aesthetics is interpreted as a leap into irrationality. For example, if modernity derides popular religiosity as superstitious irrationality, postmodernity idealizes it as such. In both cases, we are denied our humanity by being reduced to what is but one part of our humanity, namely our affect, which is in turn pitted against intellect, as if affect and intellect were mutually contradictory. Within the context of either modernity or postmodernity, the possibility that a Latino or Latina might possess an intellect is unthinkable. For white male Anglos in the academic world, the option for irrationality may seem quite liberating; for Latinos and Latinas it can only perpetuate and reinforce the continued oppression of our people. Members of the dominant culture can afford to opt for irrationality only because their culture is already implicitly deemed to be rational. Hispanics who proclaim the death of reason, however, will be perceived as simply corroborating the dominant culture's view of Hispanic culture as, indeed, representing the death of reason insofar as that culture emphasizes (irrational) affect.[42]

---

41. Ada María Isasi-Díaz, "Toward an Understanding of *Feminismo Hispano* in the U.S.A.," *Women's Consciousness, Women's Conscience,* 55.

42. *See note 38 above; Goizueta, "Theology as Intellectually Vital Inquiry."*

By grounding our theology in the praxis of U.S. Hispanic communities, U.S. Hispanic theologians seek to articulate the profound rationality of that praxis, including its communal and aesthetic dimensions. Consequently, we affirm reason and the possibility of rational discourse, but we reject the modern/postmodern dichotomy between praxis and theory. We affirm social situatedness, but we reject the assertion that social situation implies the death of the subject. Modernity proclaims the emergence of the individual, rational subject in the face of a pejoratively irrational community and tradition (understood as intergenerational community); postmodernity proclaims the death of the individual, rational subject in the face of an admirably irrational intersubjectivity. Against both modernity and postmodernity, U.S. Hispanics proclaim that community, or solidarity, is the very basis and ontological precondition for the emergence of the individual, rational subject.

In important ways, the challenge that all U.S. Hispanics represent for modern/postmodern dualisms is even more acutely visible in the experience of U.S. Hispanic women. If Hispanics have traditionally suffered from being identified exclusively with affect, feelings, sensuality, and community Hispanic women have suffered doubly from this distorting and dehumanizing identification, for they have been denied their intellect, and thus their full humanity, not only as Hispanics, but also as women. If U.S. Hispanic theologians are to avoid assimilating the same bourgeois, sentimentalized sense of community and aesthetics that permeates the dominant culture, our attempts to articulate the rationality of grounding theology in praxis, as communal and aesthetic, must look first to the experience of women, who have both maintained alive the communal and aesthetic sensibilities of our people and yet suffered from the demands of a romanticized community, aesthetics, and popular religiosity.[43]

For an example of the significance of social situatedness for theological method, see Kline Taylor, Remembering Esperanza.

43. For a discussion of the ambiguous impact that popular religiosity

U.S. Hispanic Theology as Theology

Insofar as praxis, as communal and aesthetic, is also rational, it implies not only the possibility and obligation of ethical-political action, but also the possibility and obligation of rational discourse. If reflection is intrinsic to praxis, then rational discourse is intrinsic to intersubjective action.[44] For U.S. Hispanic theologians—indeed, for all theologians—this means that our theological enterprise, whether as professionals, Christians, or, simply, human beings, is intrinsic to our praxis as U.S. Hispanics. To argue that our theology must be grounded in the praxis of our communities is, thus, to insist that the wisdom of those communities be brought into critical dialogue with the

surrounding the symbol of Mary has had on women, see, e.g., Ana María Bidegain, "Women and the Theology of Liberation," in *Through Her Eyes: Women's Theology from Latin America*, ed. Elsa Tamez (Maryknoll, N.Y.: Orbis Books, 1989), 15–36. That Mary has nevertheless remained a strong source of empowerment for many Latinas is reflected in some of the interviews conducted by Isasi-Díaz and Tarango with Hispanic women, recounted in *Hispanic Women*. See, e.g., the interview with Lupe, in which she movingly describes her devotion to Our Lady of Guadalupe (pp. 28–32). The authors observe that all of the interviews reflect the centrality of community and aesthetics to the experience of Latinas. On the importance of women's experience for theological method, see also Elsa Tamez, *Teólogos de la liberación hablan sobre la mujer* (San José, Costa Rica: DEI, 1986); Tamez, ed. *Through Her Eyes;* María Pilar Aquino, ed., *Aportes para una teología desde la mujer* (Madrid: Biblia y Fe, 1988); Aquino, *Nuestro clamor por la vida: Teología latinoamericana desde la perspectiva de la mujer* (San José, Costa Rica: DEI, 1992); and Kline Taylor, *Remembering Esperanza*, esp. 76–149. On the consequences for women of the sentimentalization of community, see Elizabeth Fox-Genovese, *Feminism without Illusions* (Chapel Hill, N.C.: University of North Carolina Press, 1991), 33–54; on the dangers of sentimentalized community more generally, see Michael J. Sandel, *Liberalism and the Limits of Justice* (Cambridge: Cambridge University Press, 1982), 147–54.

44. See Jürgen Habermas, *Legitimation Crisis* (Boston: Beacon Press, 1975); Helmut Peukert, *Science, Action, and Fundamental Theology: Toward a Theology of Communicative Action* (Cambridge, Mass.: MIT Press, 1984), esp. 163–245; Bernstein, *Beyond Objectivism and Relativism*, esp. 171–231; and Sandel, *Liberalism and the Limits of Justice*, 172–73.

larger society. Again, if U.S. Hispanics fail to engage the larger dialogue, we reinforce the dominant culture's suspicion that we have failed to do so because we cannot do so—that we lack the rational capacity. As U.S. Hispanic theologians, we must be willing to engage the dominant theological paradigms in order, precisely, to critique them. To fail to do so would be to fail to ground theology in praxis—understood now not as opposed to reason but as grounding, and thus embracing, reason dialectically, or critically.[45]

Our claims on the theological establishment are not pastoral but theological: the admission of U.S. Hispanics into the broader theological dialogue is important, not because such inclusion would be the Christian thing to do (though that is also true), but because it would be the theologically and intellectually responsible thing to do. If the inherently communal character of historical praxis implies the obligation to engage in dialogue, it likewise implies the possibility of common understanding and interpretation.[46] To marginalize some voices, such as those of U.S. Hispanics, by excluding them from the possibility of rational discourse is to undermine our common enterprise of understanding and interpretation.

This is the danger of categorizing our theology as "U.S. Hispanic theology." Too often so-called contextual theologies are dismissed as irrelevant to the larger, presumably noncontextual and hence universal, theological enterprise. U.S. Hispanic theology is then perceived as important for U.S. Hispanics, feminist theology for women, African American theology for African Americans, and so on, but none of these is considered important for the task of those who do white, male, Anglo American theology. Thus, for example, a university with no Hispanic

45. Our theology would thus be an example of what Lamb refers to as "critical praxis correlation"; see *Solidarity with Victims*, 82–88.
46. See Sandel, *Liberalism and the Limits of Justice*, 147–83, and Habermas, *Legitimation Crisis*, 110.

76

Protestants / graphluh !!

students is not likely to hire a U.S. Hispanic theologian, since the assumption is that, in that context, he or she would have no one with whom to speak, no one who would be interested in listening, and no one who would have anything to learn from the theologian. The terms *U.S. Hispanic theology* and *U.S. Hispanic theologian* are appropriate only if we are clear that these are but shorthand ways of saying that a U.S. Hispanic theologian is a theologian who does theology from a self-consciously U.S. Hispanic perspective rather than from an unconsciously Anglo American perspective.

The ontological priority of community revealed in U.S. Hispanic praxis suggests, as we have seen, that all of us are particular manifestations of an organic whole before we are individual entities: community—ultimately, the entire human community—is mediated by the particularity of individual identity. This fact anticipates, as we have also seen, both the possibility of ethical-political action and the possibility of rational discourse. The ontological priority of community implies that the theological reflection of U.S. Hispanics is important, not only because there happen to be Hispanics in our churches, our seminaries, or our universities, but also because, inasmuch as every culture and every individual is a unique and particular manifestation of the whole human community, the theology of Hispanics has significance for the whole theological community. It is by being self-consciously faithful to the particularity of our own experience as U.S. Hispanics that we are faithful to the larger human community. Consequently, it is by being faithful to our identity as U.S. Hispanic theologians that we are faithful to the larger theological community.

4

Doing Theology from the Perspective of Latin American Women

María Pilar Aquino

Before developing the topic of this chapter,[1] it would be helpful to clarify two points. The first has to do with the perspective from which we offer these reflections. We assume, as a basic presupposition, that every kind of human thought maintains an intrinsic relation to the historical context in which it originates and to which it seeks to respond, whether to transform or to legitimize that context. Theology is not exempt from this principle, even when one acknowledges the internal structure of theology as a discipline that reflects upon the experience of faith in the light of revelation. This is so because theology, "try as it might to flee from historical reality and to isolate itself in

1. I want to express my gratitude to Roberto Goizueta for translating this article from Spanish to English. These reflections were initially formulated during the Conference on the Situation of Women in Latin America, which took place in San José, Costa Rica, in July 1989, sponsored by the Ecumenical Department of Research (DEI). I want to express my deep gratitude to the DEI, the organizers of the conference, and the participants.

inter-religious discourse," as J. J. Tamayo-Acosta indicates, "always performs a historical function and enters into a relationship with the surrounding culture. At times it is offering resistance to the new cultural categories and legitimizing the established order against which these struggle for a new order. At other times, it is receiving with approval the new cultural climates, reformulating the faith in accord with these new climates, exercising a critical and evangelical function, and making possible or supporting changes in the direction of greater justice."[2]

In this sense, the theology articulated from the perspective of women commits itself to the needs, interests, and hopes of oppressed women who join their energies to those of other women and men in the construction of new social and ecclesial realities where egalitarian participation, human integrity, and life for all will be possible and where women and men will be able to realize their full potential, thus foreshadowing the New Creation already initiated by Jesus Christ. Our reflection is based on women's physical and spiritual experiences of oppression-liberation; it understands the historical present as the place where God's manifestation takes place, and it wants to respond to that manifestation within the horizon of the Christian faith. We are thus speaking here of a task that is undertaken out of the experience of those Christian communities that struggle for their liberation and for an end to the age-old history of exploitation, colonial oppression, increasing impoverishment, and inhuman subjugation to which the great majority of Latin Americans, especially women, are exposed. The existence of these women is also affected by the patriarchal structures and the systemic machismo that relegate them to a subordinate place. This clarification will help the reader understand the framework and emphases of our contribution to the issue at hand.

2. J. J. Tamayo-Acosta, *Para comprender la Teología de la Liberación* (Estella, Spain: Verbo Divino, 1989), 53.

The second point refers to the limits and challenges one confronts when doing theology from the perspective of women. Since this is a perspective only recently explored in the history of the church and theology, we believe that in our context, though there have already been significant contributions, this is a task yet to be more fully undertaken. We Latin American women ought to engage in this task with all our energies alongside women from every corner of the earth since we share the most profound longings of the oppressed in their eagerness to renew all things (2 Cor. 5:17); that is, to incorporate in the social and ecclesial orders and in the processes of knowledge the constitutive expression of humanity: women and men, both destined to enjoy the fullness of life in communion with the earth and with the whole of creation.

The Intelligibility of Faith from the Perspective of Women

A statement by I. Gebara accurately expresses the traditional attitude of the church and theology with respect to women: "The representatives of religious power believe that they know God's will as regards men and, especially, women. But God's love will not be limited. It is found where one least expects to find it."[3] This being so, Latin American women today no longer expect others to guide and define their experience of life and faith, rather they seek to define themselves and to express their own experience and their hopes in their own words. It is already widely acknowledged that traditional theology offers few possibilities for women to participate as subjects in the theological enterprise, given its male-centered and sexist character. Therefore, the finest currents of theological reflection done from the perspective of women—widely known as feminist theology—

---

3. I. Gebara, "La opción por el pobre como opción por la mujer pobre," *Concilium* 214 (1987): 472.

achieve their self-understanding within the framework of liberation theology.[4] It is liberation theology that has, in fact, made possible a new space and new perspectives so that women will articulate their theological word from their own context, out of their own consciousness and their own condition as women.[5] In effect, the theology of liberation sinks its roots in the experience of an impoverished and believing people that has experienced the power of the Spirit and has raised itself up over the course of a long period of captivity in order to forge a path toward a new order in which life will be possible. For women, as a fundamental part of the ecclesial community and as an essential subject within the people as a whole, it is not only possible but necessary to articulate the intelligibility of faith out of their own experience, to allow theology itself to acknowledge the great riches of the people of God and to activate the anticipation of new realities congruent with the liberating Christian vision. To subsume or ignore the perspective of women would serve to reproduce the systems that legitimize male superiority,

4. This posture is common to the theological reflection of the First and Third Worlds. For theology from the perspective of Third World women, compare, V. Fabella and M. A. Oduyoye, eds., *With Passion and Compassion: Third World Women Doing Theology* (Maryknoll, N.Y.: Orbis Books, 1988); Tamez, *Through Her Eyes; Las mujeres toman la palabra* (San José, Costa Rica: DEI, 1989); Aquino, *Nuestro clamor por la vida.* From among the vast literature in First World feminist theology, see Letty Russell, *Human Liberation in a Feminist Perspective* (Philadelphia: Westminster, 1974); Carol P. Christ and Judith Plaskow, eds., *Womanspirit Rising: A Feminist Reader in Religion* (New York: Harper & Row, 1979); Catherine Halkes, "Feminist Theology: An Interim Assessment," *Concilium* 134 (1980), 110-23; Elisabeth Schüssler Fiorenza, *In Memory of Her: A Feminist Theological Reconstruction of Christian Origins* (New York: Crossroad, 1985); Rosemary Radford Ruether, *Sexism and God-Talk: Toward a Feminist Theology* (Boston: Beacon Press, 1983); Patricia Wilson-Kastner, *Faith, Feminism, and the Christ* (Philadelphia: Fortress Press, 1983); E. Moltmann-Wendel, *A Land Flowing with Milk and Honey: Perspectives on Feminist Theology* (New York: Crossroad, 1988); Anne E. Carr, *Transforming Grace: Christian Tradition and Women's Experience* (San Francisco: Harper & Row, 1988).
5. M. C. Bingemer, interviewed in Tamez, *Teólogos de la liberación*, 131.

the unequal division of social and religious labor based on gender, and the denial of the physical, psychological, and spiritual integrity of women.

On the other hand, Latin American women doing theology of liberation attempt to recover a right that has been usurped: the right to reflect upon their unique way of experiencing revelation and living their faith as a liberating force rather than as a source of oppression. They want to recover the right to express their experience of faith out of the integrity of their being so that the theological intelligence in its configuration, structure, method, and contents will promote the fulfillment of women as subjects in their own right. This enterprise, though not unique to women, is required of them in the face of the male-centered focus of the theology currently articulated by men, including those who take a liberationist perspective.

Immersed in a reality in which women are oppressed in many ways, doing theology is not a luxury, but a necessity and a right to be reclaimed. It is a necessity because Latin American Christian women are convinced that their faith has something to say about their oppressive situation. Neither God, nor the egalitarian praxis of Jesus, nor the gospel's liberating message, nor a sizable segment of the ecclesial community remain passive before the immeasurable suffering inflicted on them. It is a right to be reclaimed because it concerns a right that has been usurped and denied over the centuries of the history of the church and theology: that of articulating the intelligibility of the faith out of Latin American women's situation of impoverishment, out of their situation as oppressed women seeking transformation, and out of their experience of faith alongside a struggling people. It concerns, in short, the reappropriation of their right to the word itself.

We are speaking here of an integral perspective from which men and women can and should reflect on the faith if they want to overcome the exclusivism and partiality of the male-centered point of view. With their contribution, women propose to make explicit the experiences and knowledge of women that lead toward the anticipation of new social and ecclesial realities that will benefit women and men. The feminist theological task of Latin American women acquires its own unique features not only because it reflects the novelty of she who theologizes— the heretofore silent woman—but also because of its perception of what is real and the emphasis it places on the problems to be resolved, an emphasis not always made explicit by male-centered reflection. And *the way* in which women do theological reflection is not always the same as that traditionally exercised by men in their theologizing. There exist, therefore, distinct features we should identify concerning content and method. For now, let us address the following five issues.

Who Theologizes?

Latin American women, who for centuries have been silenced and subsumed into the history of the church and theology, now recover their right to exercise their theological intelligence.[6] As women, they have been relegated to a subordinate position, excluded from theological education, from knowledge and skills, and from the sacred ministry, the symbolic and sacramental expression of the faith. Throughout history, but even more so today, they resist becoming that which the culture, religion, and patriarchal society have decided they ought to be. Women understand that the inherited stereotypes created for them are foreign to their own consciousness and identity as women. They accept, on the contrary, the great challenge of naming their own countenance, and they seek new paths of

6. It is absurd that after five hundred years of Christianity on this continent, there are less than eight Latin American women holding the doctoral degree in theology.

cooperation, solidarity, and life.[7] As Elsa Tamez observes, it appears that we are passing from "the certain" to "the uncertain" and from the uncertain to the possible.[8]

From Where Does the Latin American Woman Theologize?

Theological reflection from the perspective of Latin American women takes as its starting point "our experience of faith, lived from the underside of power and authority, . . . the cry of women comes from within the massive cry of the poor and oppressed, in the midst of the exploitation and misery in which the majority of the population lives. And this is why theological reflection from a woman's point of view wishes to make its voice heard as a service to all of those alienated from society."[9] Latin American women do theology out of their age-old conviction that God is on their side and that it is by the power of the Spirit that today they raise themselves up in order to leap from individualism to the life of community and to experience solidarity and communion with other oppressed women.

This theology is elaborated by these women in order to transform and overcome the asymmetrical relations that condemn them to a subordinate position and to inhumanity, to heal their wounds, to recover their self-esteem, and to regain their own values. The women's theological task is, likewise, undertaken from within a profound desire to be the church; it articulates the truths of the faith in intimate connection with the commitments and activities of those poor and believing women who, in the base ecclesial communities, make the church a real community of egalitarian discipleship.

7. N. Ritchie, "Mujer y Cristología," ed. Elsa Tamez, *El rostro femenino de la teología* (San José, Costa Rica: DEI,1986), 120; I. Gebara, "La mujer hace teología: Un ensayo para la reflexión," in ibid., 13–17.

8. Tamez, "La fuerza del desnudo," Tamez, ed., *El rostro femenino*, 196.

9. A. M. Tepedino, "Feminist Theology as the Fruit of Passion and Compassion," in Fabella and Oduyoye, *With Passion and Compassion*, 165.

What Is the Object of Her Reflection?

Like all Christian theology, the feminist theological perspective of Latin American women seeks to confront the problems and challenges of its own reality. It is, therefore, interested in articulating a critical reflection upon the physical and spiritual transformative experiences of oppressed women, in which God's liberating activity is recognized, in order to contribute to the process of their own liberation as well as the liberation of their people. Because of this emphasis, and this way of appropriating reality to constitute itself, this theology helps to enrich, broaden, and deepen the hermeneutical horizon of the theology of liberation itself.

The perspective of women makes explicit the self-communication of God, which is discovered especially in the experience of women's oppression and liberation. No activity that has to do with the creation, re-creation, and defense of life-giving systems conducive to human integrity can be theologically insignificant for this particular manner of understanding God's self-revelation. The reason is that the activities undertaken by oppressed women to ensure their own survival, as well as that of their dependents (children, the elderly, the sick), bear inherently the seal of compassion, solidarity, justice, liberty, love for the poor, and a high degree of courage and strength.[10] These activities are related to the contents of faith and are the primary font that nourishes the theological task of women.

Likewise, Latin American women reflect upon the way in which power is exercised in society and in the church, upon the sexual division of social labor based on the separation of the public from the private sphere, upon what the relations between women and men are and could be, upon those divisions in the

10. These are some signs of how near and present God's reign is in history. See J. B. Libanio and M. C. Bingemer, *Escatología Cristiana* (Madrid: Ediciones Paulinas, 1985), 123–41, 280–81.

Christian community that do not contribute to the unity of the people of God, and upon their own devastated corporal existence. In dialogue with the liberating Christian traditions, they reflect on all of this with the intention of helping to overcome the structures and systems that impede their self-actualization as historical subjects in their own right, in society and the church.

How Do Women Do Theology?

Women combine different ways of talking about God. They seek "always to begin with lived experience . . . which, as a consequence, leads to the rejection of abstract language in the face of life and in the face of those things that touch the very depths of human relationships . . . living reality is the point of departure of a more systematic theological explanation."[11] In fact, in the face of the word-centered character of traditional theology, the feminist theology of liberation manifests itself in a more praxis-based and contextual character.[12] Precisely because of its word-centered emphasis, traditional theology often became reduced to knowledge for the sake of knowledge and to the reasoned word that clarifies and defines truths. Within this mode of theologizing, every other kind of human access to God's truth and every other word was considered false and inconsistent, thus closing off the possibility of any other type of knowledge and access to other dimensions of the divine reality. In this process, not only was theology, as *intellectus fidei,* distorted, so too was the very reality of God. But it turns out that this word was only the logos of the white, male, Western colonial culture— later, the order of patriarchal imperialistic capitalism. It turned into an elitist discourse that excluded other words that did not faithfully repeat or speak its language, such as the words of

11. I. Gebara, interviewed in Tamez, *Teólogos de la liberación,* 122.
12. For a discussion of the logocentric character of traditional theology, see Tamez, "La fuerza del desnudo," *Teólogos de la liberación,* 173.

impoverished women of a subordinate race. A monologue was thus established among men, but no dialogue was established between women and men as a diverse human totality.[13] The theological intelligence, as exercised by women, distances itself from abstract and rationalist discourse detached from what is real of reality—that is, the cry of the suffering majority of humanity in its historical present—in order to allow theology to communicate in the diverse languages of faith as a response to God's present activities in the struggles and resistance of the poor and oppressed. It thus includes a conscious option for a way of exercising intelligence that dynamically articulates life and thought.

> The passionate and compassionate way in which women do theology is a rich contribution to theological science. The key to this theological process is the word *life*. . . . Women are deeply covenanted with life, giving life and protecting life. . . . In doing theology, we . . . find ourselves committed and faithful to all the vital elements that compose human life. Thus without losing its scientific seriousness, which includes analyzing the basic causes of women's multiple oppression, our theologizing is deeply rooted in experience, in affect, in life. We as women feel called to do scientific theology passionately, a theology based in *feeling as well as on knowledge*, on wisdom as well as on science, a theology done not only with the mind but also with the heart, the body, the womb. We consider this a challenge and an imperative not only for theology done from the perspective of women, but also for all theology.[14]

Therefore, in elaborating its theological discourse, the perspective of women does not reject reason, which is intrinsic to humanity; rather, it places the logos and its function in a new

13. M. C. Bingemer, "Chairete: Alegrai-vos (Lc 15, 8–10)," in *A Mulher no futuro da teología da libertaçao*, Revista Eclesiástica Brasileira 48/191 (1988), 570–75.

14. "Final Document: Intercontinental Women's Conference" (Oaxtepec, México, Dec. 1–6, 1986), in Fabella and Oduyoye, *With Passion and Compassion*, 188 (emphasis mine).

light where the man is not the possessor of reason, par excellence, and the logos is not the fundamental and only valid mediation of theology.[15] There exist other languages which, even
when not recognized as authentic theological categories, are also
appropriate means used by oppressed women for expressing the
truths of the Christian faith based on the experience of their
struggle for survival and defense of life.[16] These languages include: the testimonial, narrative, or oral tradition; knowledge
through wisdom; poetry; recreation; the many forms of expression through gesture; and songs of hope, lament, denun-
ciation, and consolation.[17] These are, therefore, important
sources that liberation theology cannot disregard. The feminist
theological task grounded in Latin American women's experience and knowledge acquires vitality precisely from its capacity
to enter into dialogue with gestures, symbols, religious expressions, traditions, memory, and the traditional language of
our people, which oppressed women have known how to preserve in the midst of their resistance and struggles against the
many forms of subordination and colonization.[18] C. del Prado
suggests that, in this universe of new languages, "we never
exhaust our understanding of reality, which always appears as
new and engaging."[19] It is not surprising, then, that the theology

15. Tamayo-Acosta, *Para comprender*, 131.

16. For discussions of the diverse languages of theology from the perspective of women, see, Gebara, "La mujer hace teología"; Tamez, "La fuerza
del desnudo," 193.

17. Gebara, "La mujer hace teología," 19–20. The same observation was
made during the DEI's Latin American conference on the situation of women,
San José, Costa Rica (1989).

18. See A. Lapiedra, "Religiosidad popular y mujer andina," in *El rostro
Femenino*, 49–72; M. T. Porcile, "El derecho a la belleza en América Latina,"
in ibid., 85–107. See also T. Cavalcanti, "Sobre la participación de las mujeres
en el VI Encuentro Intereclesial de las Comunidades de Base," ed. Aquino,
Aportes para una teología desde la mujer, 128–44.

19. C. del Padro, "Yo siento a Dios de otro modo," ed. Tamez, "*El rostro
Femenino*," 80.

articulated by women will lead to the renewal not only of liberation theology done by men, but of theology in general.

To What End Do Women Theologize?

A fundamental presupposition of the theological task undertaken by women from their own point of view is, as M. C. Bingemer indicates, that "the most important thing is not the theological discourse of women, or the words they speak, but the liberation which ought to take place and in the process of which theology plays a role and has a specific identity."[20] In short, the principal basis for understanding the intention of the feminist theological task of Latin American women is the emphasis on praxis over abstract knowledge; that is, the transformation of reality over its mere explanation. That task seeks to help affirm women as subjects in their own right with the ability to make decisions concerning their own destiny, physical and spiritual, as well as that of their people. "We are aware that our liberation is part and parcel of the liberation of all the poor and oppressed promised by the gospel. Our efforts are rooted in Scripture. Our creation in God's image demands a total rupture with the prevailing patriarchal system in order to build an egalitarian society."[21] That is why women propose the eradication of those structures that generate massive poverty, systematic death, and immense inhuman suffering so that the fullness of life, justice, and liberation will become possible.

The perspective of women does not understand itself as a liberating process apart from other popular social movements that also seek to construct an egalitarian order, but it does demand that the liberation of the poor not be undertaken at the expense of the subordination of women; therefore the itinerary

20. M. C. Bingemer, "Teología del Tercer Mundo," *Concilium* 219 (1988): 307.
21. "Final Document," 147.

of women includes a global liberation and a specific one, simultaneously and equally articulated. The theologizing of women is inspired by the vision of the new world desired by God for the whole of humanity and seeks to foreshadow, through the commitment to justice, the fullness of life promised by God for the whole of creation.

The perspective of women accords priority to the achievement of women's human integrity and emphasizes the right of full humanity for all women and men. We thus propose to "deepen our commitment and our work of solidarity with a view toward a full humanity for all . . . as part of our commitment to total liberation and the achievement of the full humanity of all: women and men alike."[22] It is even more necessary to affirm this aspect since we find ourselves immersed in the structures of patriarchal, imperialistic capitalism, whose prejudicial effects are manifested not only in increasing poverty, but also in the profound dehumanization into which whole peoples are dragged.

The commitment to human integrity is also undertaken within the church because women understand that we cannot recover the fullness of life for ourselves and for all people if that fullness does not become real in the Christian community in all its dimensions, in emulation of the egalitarian community constituted by Jesus and his movement.[23] In an ecclesial reality where women continue to be excluded from decisionmaking, from access to theological formation, and from the sacred ministry, a theology from the perspective of women "urgently calls for sustained efforts to discover new ways of being church, of being in the world as the visible presence of God's reign and of the new creation. . . . Our faith in the power of the cross and the resurrection empowers us to live out the vision of *God's new*

22. Ibid., 184.
23. For the notion of an egalitarian discipleship, see the illuminating contribution of Schüssler Fiorenza, *In Memory of Her*, 105ff.

creation, where no one is subordinated or enslaved, but where free people take part in God's liberating project to build a true community and a new society."[24]

This proposal for a renewed church is born in the actual experience of innumerable women who, throughout the continent and the Caribbean, are reinventing the church in Christian communities. We are concerned with re-creating the unity of the people of God in order to overcome divisions of class, race, gender, religious confessions, and social status without overlooking the internal divisions that resist the creative work of the Spirit. The feminist theology of liberation articulated by Latin American women is, therefore, profoundly ecumenical.[25]

Another aspect has to do with the reconstruction of the harmony between humanity and the earth.[26] T. Cavalcanti observes that, ever since peoples have been aware of their existence, "women have had a special, intimate relationship with the earth. The earth divulges secrets to women, and between women and the earth there is a mysterious relationship."[27] The rupture of this harmonious relationship results from the abuse of power inherent in the patriarchal system because this power is exercised

24. "Final Document," 145.
25. In fact, the vitality of liberation theology from the perspective of Latin American and Third World women also issues from this characteristic. Ecumenism is a particular and specific characteristic not only of women's theologizing, but of liberation theology in general. Cf. *Teología desde el Tercer Mundo: Documentos Finales de los cinco congresos internacionales de la Asociación Ecuménica de Teólogos del Tercer Mundo (EATWOT)* (San José, Costa Rica: DEI, 1982). For a relevant contribution to the topic of ecumenism in Latin America, see J. De Santa Ana, *Ecumenismo y Liberación* (Madrid: Ediciones Paulinas, 1987). For this theologian, the divisions between men and women are a serious threat to the unity of the people of God (see pp. 61–68). C. Alvarez made similar observations during the conference on the situation of women in Latin America (DEI, 1989).
26. For important reflections on this aspect, see T. Cavalcanti, "Produzindo Teología no Feminino Plural: a Propósito do III Encontro Nacional de Teología na perspectiva da mulher," *Perspectiva Teología* 20 (1988), 362ff.
27. Ibid., 362.

within a logic of domination rather than one of solidarity and mutual respect. Women know that their liberation is, in itself, related to the liberation of the earth because the promotion and defense of life is related to both. "Only on a socialized earth, with all its products redistributed, can women beget communitarian women and men, new generations living in freedom and solidarity, as was the dream of Mary (Luke 1:49-53). The attempt to readjust the relations between the earth, men, and women retrieves the biblical project of social organization, modeled after the face of God, and barely visible in a harmoniously organized humanity (Gen 1:27)."[28]

Finally, we want to underscore another fundamental intent of the theology done by women. If the perspective of women carries a strong element of hope and utopia, so too does that dimension that seeks to recover our own past by reappropriating the ancestral wisdom of whole peoples and an infinite number of women who have preceded us in the struggle for a more just world. T. Cavalcanti indicates that "poor women have maintained alive the memory of the past."[29] Certainly this has been the case. For this reason, we want to turn in another direction and open our ears to the barely audible but not silenced word of the women who have preceded us, not only in order to reveal and enlighten the roots of our own being and go in search of our original identity, but also to reconstruct that which was their hope and which, beyond the frontiers of space and time, gives meaning to the liberating struggles of women today. Neither violent conquest, nor repeated colonization—first, Hispanic-Iberian, and now Anglo-Saxon—nor patriarchal, imperialistic capitalism, nor sexist clericalism have been able to erase from the face of the earth the living memory of innumerable women who have retained the hope of realizing their own destiny. These

28. Ibid., 363.
29. T. Cavalcanti, "Sobre la participación de las mujeres," 135.

women have struggled and offered their lives for the gospel's "better part" and for that which is most precious in our ancient cultures.[30]

The enormous capacity of poor and oppressed women for resistance and for affirming the priority of life even in the midst of the shadows to which they were condemned is not, to be certain, inherited from the colonizing peoples who have set themselves forth as the paradigm of humanity par excellence. In the name of that paradigm the colonizers did not hide their intention of eradicating from the face of the earth all those peoples who would resist assimilation—the native indigenous peoples, blacks, and women. On the contrary, the capacity for resistance and for affirming life are the legacy of the ancient, disinherited peoples, destined for dehumanization, who have bequeathed to us their most intimate solidarity as an instrument of survival and as a deeply rooted attitude toward others in the face of modern-day colonizers. Women have had to learn to live in this profound solidarity, an attitude the European-Iberian and Anglo-Saxon cultures have been unable to engender. For these cultures, the division of the Latin American peoples is the best instrument for perpetuating their domination.

In sum, to what end do Latin American women theologize? We want to recover the value of the experience and knowledge of poor and oppressed women in order to affirm their place as rightful subjects in history, society, the church, and theology. We want to re-create our own history alongside the struggles and hopes of the great suffering majority of humankind; as Elsa Tamez says, "to cultivate history with new hands, new seeds, new concerns, and new weapons. To produce new fruits, new relationships, new ways of practicing the faith in the church, and a new theological discourse."[31]

---

30. On the role of "subversive memory" in our context, see R. Vidales, *Utopía y Liberación: El amanecer del indio* (San José, Costa Rica: DEI, 1988).
31. Tamez, "La fuerza del desnudo," 202.

The Point of Departure for Women Doing Theology

Latin American feminist liberation theology assumes the option for the poor as its hermeneutical perspective and the social location for its theological task. This option is the fundamental and necessary principle for articulating the intelligibility of faith in a way that will remain open to the actual reality and the divine manifestation it contains. The existence of massive poverty, the immeasurable suffering of whole peoples, and the longstanding oppression of women cannot but influence this theology at its very core. The option for the poor is demanded by reality itself and represents the necessary, honest, and appropriate response to reality. At a more fundamental level, such an option is demanded by the sources of biblical liberating traditions, the praxis of Jesus, the early Christian movement, and the prophetic movements that have occurred in the history of church and society. As an enterprise that articulates the language of faith, theology from the perspective of women understands itself as tied to the great current of popular social movements that seek to eradicate existing inequalities; it is based in the experiences of this people in search of alternative realities and seeks to contribute, from the horizon of the Christian faith, to this people's liberating journey.

However, liberation theology from the perspective of women privileges and deepens one dimension of the option for the poor; it attends to the questions, the historical and spiritual experiences, the understanding, the memory, and the aspirations and hopes of poor and oppressed women in their search for transformation. It attends to these aspects of women's existence not only as part of the impoverished and believing majority, but first and foremost *as women*, as a concrete visage among the poor that can no longer be relegated to the shadows, and as a collective subject that experiences, in many forms, a profound oppression that injures them, the society, theology, and the church.[32]

Consequently, for a theology to express the interests, aspirations, and hopes of women, the option for the poor takes the form of an option for the impoverished and oppressed woman who has been forced by the male-centered, patriarchal world to bargain away and justify her own humanity and whose spiritual experience and systematic articulation have been wrested from her. I. Gebara asserts that, in the Latin American context,

the poor have many faces: laborers, farmworkers, beggars, abandoned children, the marginalized and dispossessed youth, and others. They are men and women, but among them we should give precedence to one group: *the women.* . . . The poor woman today is poor even among the poor. She is truly other: the overburdened woman, the menstruating woman, the laboring woman, mother, daughter, and wife. She is, at the same time, both subject and object of our option for the poor.[33]

Latin American women are oppressed in many forms because of the diversity inherent in the polymorphous power of patriarchal, imperialistic capitalism. In a system based on asymmetrical relations of class, gender, and race, no allowance is made for the existence of otherness or for a dialogue among equals. Here, impoverished black, mestiza, Latina, and indigenous women are forced to take a subordinate place. Furthermore, this system, which is often supported by the churches, has defined for women and men distinct social roles and has sought to socially transform as a disadvantage and weakness the power of women, including their capacity for reproduction, the expression of their sexuality, their deepest desires, and even their hopes.

This situation is especially difficult for Latin American women. In the first place, they share with other women throughout

32. The term "profound oppression" in reference to women is that of Gutiérrez, interviewed in Tamez, *Teólogos de la liberación*, 52.
33. Gebara, "La opción por el pobre," 467–68 (emphasis mine).

the world the common experience of oppression because of their gender. In the second place, the great majority of Latin American women belong to the impoverished sectors of society, the great suffering majority of humankind. This fact already establishes a substantial difference with respect to the subordinate position they share with women from the dominant sectors who live in contexts of privilege. This fundamental difference becomes evident, above all, in everyday life; the vital necessities and the struggles that they face are different for each group of women.[34] The struggles of the impoverished and oppressed Latin American women concern their very survival and that of their children, whereas the struggles of women who live in comfort concern the interests of well-being congruent with their social status.

In their struggles, First World women do not always make explicit the causal connection between the living conditions of each group. They attenuate the global connection between the social locations, and they obscure the fact that the survival of Third World women can only take place at the expense of the privileges of First World women. One has to ask how the theological discourse of women relates, to a greater or lesser degree, to this problematic situation. The theology elaborated by Latinas in North America cannot evade this question for four reasons. First, if the causal connections of social location are not established, the epistemological location fails to yield any fruit, and

---

34. Rosemary Radford Ruether addresses this issue as follows: "Upper class, white women easily fall into an abstract analysis of women's 'oppressed' status that ignores the privileges of their own class and race. When this occurs, their movement fails to connect with the women of oppressed groups. Their movement turns into an upper class, white women's movement that fails to go beyond the demand for privileges proportionate to those enjoyed by the men of their own group, forgetting the unjust racism and the class context of those privileges." See Ruether, *Mujer Nueva-Tierra Nueva: La liberación del hombre y la mujer en un mundo renovado* (Buenos Aires: Megápolis, 1977), 46.

hence a discourse is created that has little possibility of promoting the common liberation of women. Second, this aspect is not made explicit in the theology done by men; consequently, it should be emphasized by women, among other reasons, because of the intimate solidarity that exists among women and because of the necessity of incorporating the reality of the suffering world in the theological discourse. In the third place, even when women share in the oppression of the majority, they will bear the brunt of the oppression. This means that they are oppressed not only as women, but also as part of the subordinate race and as part of the impoverished peoples, and even within these, the woman bears the heaviest burden.[35] The relationship of women and men among the poor is not exempt from asymmetry because the oppressed man continues to be *machista* and, as such, continues to be a male oppressor.[36] In the fourth place, the oppression of women becomes complex when the dimension of race is introduced because the indigenous, black, and mestizo woman should seek to reformulate the dominant Western stereotype that legitimizes the superiority of the white race.

Our womanhood is not a weakness, nor is it a disadvantage, as patriarchal imperialistic capitalism and sexist clericalism would have us believe; rather it is our strength. Our womanhood is not a source of weakness, as the male-centered system asserts; rather it is the rich source of a re-creative spirituality, perseverance, resistance, solidarity, and the assumption of responsibility in defense of life. This life-giving logic emerges from the depths of our being. In this sense, Gebara underscores some fundamental elements that should be emphasized in the option for women:

(1) The option for the poor is not an option extrinsic to ourselves, and neither is the option for women. We are concerned with forging a path, from within, that will make possible

35. See the suggestive reflections of H. Assmann in Tamez, *Teólogos de la liberación*, 41–43.
36. Ibid.

the reconstruction of women's own internal unity. For this to occur, the fundamental step is the *option of the woman for herself.* This is an invitation to women to accept and embrace themselves, before all else, as women and to rediscover their source of strength in an ongoing process.

(2) The internal journey toward the rediscovery of the interior source and a reencounter with their own roots represents the first step toward an openness to others. Women discover themselves in relation to other subjects who should also experience a collective rebirth and a rediscovery of themselves as a human group. The *option for others*, in itself, leads to the destruction of the barrier of fear in order to reach the frontiers of courage. Fear is broken in order to express one's own experience, which is transformed into the key experience of the Christian life: "to love others as ourselves."

(3) Both the option of women for themselves and the option for others emerge from the same source. They are but two dimensions of one single movement that should converge in the *option for a new future of love and justice.* Within a reality characterized by tremendous suffering, misery, anguish, and dehumanization, women become the "sentinels" of hope. Through their actions, motivated by faith, they engage life in anticipation of a new future, and this hope lies in the very womb of their existence as a life-giving gust of wind giving that existence direction, meaning, and depth.[37]

37. Gebara, "La opción por el pobre," 464–72.

Some Characteristics of Latin American
Feminist Theology

Some of the methodological characteristics that feminist theology from the perspective of Latin American women has developed for its task have already been articulated elsewhere.[38] Here, we are interested in highlighting some elements that this theology shares with all Christian theology, especially with the theology of liberation in general, elements that are emphasized in the perspective of women.[39] In order to do this, it is important to underscore the fact that, in its own task, the theology done by women is not a neutral endeavor. On the contrary, as we have reiterated, it emerges as a specific form of women's struggle for their right to life. With this basic presupposition in mind, we point to some of the characteristics of this theology.

First, this feminist theology does not understand itself as an enterprise in and of itself. It does not overlook the function it performs within the realm of reality in which it is elaborated. This means that liberation theology from the perspective of women is concerned with its practical impact on the reality which it proposes to engage and change. As an enterprise situated within historical coordinates, it is open to verification according to whether or not it contributes to the liberating interests of women. In this sense, feminist theology done by Latin American women is demonstrating its ability to energize the struggles of oppressed women as well as increasing their consciousness of their historical, physical, psychological, and spiritual strength. It is fostering fortitude and clarity in the

38. See, for example, "Final Statement: Latin American Conference on Theology from the Perspective of Women" (Buenos Aires, Argentina, Oct. 30–Nov. 3, 1985), in Fabella and Oduyoye, *With Passion and Compassion*, 181–83.

39. See Jon Sobrino, "Teología de la liberación y teología europea progresista," in VARIOS, *Desafíos Cristianos. Misión Abierta* (Madrid: Lóguez, 1988), 449–53.

transformative praxis of women and contributing to the reformulation of the relations that ought to exist between men and
women in the public and private spheres.

Second, this theology understands itself in reference to the
actualization of the reign of God. It seeks to contribute to the
realization of the fullness of life contained in God's salvific will;
for this reason, it commits itself to historical and transcendent
liberation. In effect, women's theological task is to be understood
as partner, ally, and mouthpiece of that multitude of oppressed
women who, from the underside of history, have experienced
the power of the Spirit and have risen to their feet. It is also to
be understood as being united to the experience of those women
who have felt the presence of God's re-creative activity in their
own lives and are willing to rewrite history; they are willing to
reread the liberating message of God's alliance with all peoples
and to reexamine Jesus Christ's redemptive act, from within
their own situation of captivity, in order to find the strength,
clarity, and paths for living and enduring their struggle.[40]

Third, this theology is willing to enter into the conflicts of
history. It is itself marked by conflict and suffering. These dimensions are intrinsic to any theological enterprise that has truly
identified with the cause of the impoverished and oppressed and
has identified with their journey and destiny. Consequently, this
theology knows that it participates in the fortunes of all who
open new paths; it suffers discredit, criticism, persecution, dis-
interest, censorship, and even a slow or violent death inflicted
by those who feel that their domination in society and the church
is threatened. For women, conflict and suffering are present
both in their theologizing and in every aspect of their existence.

Fourth, like all Christian theology, this theology lives in
intimacy with the ecclesial dimension. It cannot be any other
way, since its reflection is born out of the faith experience of

40. Bingemer, "Chairete: Alegrai-vos," 569.

women in the base communities and the various Christian communities. This theology understands itself as originating in the faith of those oppressed women who sustain the everyday life of the church of the poor. The theology from the perspective of women accords significance to the egalitarian discipleship promoted by Jesus; it seeks to recover the oldest biblical and ecclesial liberating traditions in order to clarify the fundamental characteristics of that which the church is called to be. It seeks to overcome the contradictions inherent in a juridical ecclesiology (clergy-laity—sacred-profane; *ecclesia docens—ecclesia discens*) and proposes a new way of being church based on the baptismal call to a discipleship of equals in which every segment of God's people participates. We speak here of a ministerial community in which there are no subjects who occupy a subordinate place. This new way of being church yields different relations within the ecclesial community and gives rise to a new type of ecumenism.

Fifth, because of its internal dynamic, this theology engenders a spirituality in women and other segments of God's people that will nourish hope and perseverance in the midst of suffering. It activates their strength to change the present in the certainty that God is on their side. Its point of departure is oppressed women's experiences of oppression and liberation, and the theology itself becomes a spiritual experience. Women's theological task is pregnant with a spirituality of hope that is born in our situation as women and expresses strength, suffering, and gratitude.[41] Prayer and celebration are two inseparable dimensions of this particular way of understanding and articulating the faith.

As we indicated earlier, another characteristic of this theology has to do with its particular way of carrying out the process of understanding in the context of the intelligibility of faith. In the face of the rationalistic logic of Western thought and theology,

41. "Final Statement," 182.

the perspective of women articulates the logos of theology in a different way in order to allow it to integrate, into the "second act," the various dimensions of human existence; this process gives rise to a new, more holistic discourse.[42] Therefore, women's theology strives to be "unifying, bringing together different human dimensions; strength and tenderness, happiness and tears, intuition and reason."[43] It strives to overcome the monolithic character of the male-centered perspective in its one-dimensional approach to the multifaceted dynamics of life. But theology articulated by women does not assume a self-sufficient status in its method or content; on the contrary, it feels called to "carry out its discourse and reflection . . . as a humble and eager contribution to the liberation" of women and their people.[44] It is a project that serves to build up the people of God. In this sense, gratuitous love is its seal.

Finally, the last feature that we want to underscore is this theology's joyful and hopeful character, which is accentuated by its self-understanding as a companion in the struggles and hopes of oppressed women. Latin American women articulate their feminist theological perspective as *good news*. Furthermore, after centuries of exclusion, the very fact that the Latin American woman has access to theology already constitutes good news for her. In addition, this character of good news is also derived from the presuppositions and goals that this theology assumes in its own construction. It is good news for women because it emboldens them to recover their own value, strength, and self-esteem; but it is also good news for men, history, the church, and all humanity because it seeks unexplored paths that will lead to a common liberation and that will foreshadow in the

42. For an analysis of the "first act" and "second act" in liberation theology, see G. Gutiérrez, *Hablar de Dios desde el sufrimiento del inocente* (Salamanca: Sígueme, 1988), 17ff.

43. "Final Document," 205.

44. Bingemer, "Chairete: Alegrai-vos," 570.

present the fullness of life promised by God for the whole of creation.

Signs of Contention, Signs of Hope

Even though Latin American feminist liberation theology has made significant advances over the past few years, there nevertheless remain many challenges that we must confront. One of these has to do with the acknowledgment, by both men and women, of the importance of women in social and ecclesial processes of transformation. This implies, among other things, that we must promote the self-expression of women and give greater importance to their experience and knowledge in order to change what society and religion define as a disadvantage into strength and liberation. We are convinced that the contribution of women to theology and the church is crucial to strengthening local and global processes of emancipation.

There remain many conventional attitudes and conceptual systems that we ought to transform. Even when we identify with the struggle of the poor and oppressed, particularly that of women, for their liberation, we cannot lose sight of the tensions that delay the process. These include: individualistic attitudes, personality conflicts, struggles for power and control over others, sectarianism, competition among women and among different projects; an accentuated machismo in men and even in women who replicate among themselves male patterns of competition; the defense of one's position or role in the community, which prevents those who follow from occupying new positions; the rejection and refusal to acknowledge the participation of women as subjects in their own right; those forms of reductionism that overlook or postpone gender inequalities, in both theory and practice; and the masculinizing authoritarianism of women theoretically committed to the feminist vision. All these situations, as well as others not here mentioned, are added to the broader tensions of social, political, and ecclesial conflict.

Notwithstanding these signs of contention, which should still be overcome, greater still are the signs of hope on which we should focus. The light, true joy, intimate solidarity, and profound communion that are born out of the spiritual experience of the marginalized, poor, and oppressed women in their struggle for liberation fortify our desire to remain united in our convictions (1 Cor. 2:10) despite the afflictions and tribulations. The reason is that what is at stake is not the respectability of theology, nor that of theologians, but the construction of the New Earth, the New Creation in Christ, and the unity of the people of God. Hence, it is necessary to give priority to whatever makes possible the advance toward justice, liberation, and human integrity and to whatever has as its end the affirmation of women as subjects in their own right. Theological intelligence, then, serves the realization of these dimensions, so necessary in our present historical circumstances. As N. Ritchie observes, "to be witnesses to the resurrection is to reject the final victory of death, struggling against everything that places limits on the fullness of life and to be witnesses to the new life, in the midst of hopelessness and the bitter taste of defeat, proclaiming and building pathways of hope."[45]

45. N. Ritchie, "Mujer y Cristología," 124.

5

A Hispanic Approach to Trinitarian Theology:
The Dynamics of Celebration, Reflection, and Praxis

Sixto J. García

North American and Continental Trinitarian Theologies and Their Relation to Hispanic Trinitarian Perspectives

Euro-American Trinitarian Thought

The systematic theological reflections on the Trinity of European or North American origin have traditionally drawn from biblical (mostly New Testament), patristic, scholastic, and contemporary sources, mediated by the philosophical and historical categories of each age. With the advent of political theology in Europe and liberation-oriented theologies in the Third World within the last three decades, contemporary trinitarian theologies address questions formerly regarded by theologians and nontheologians alike as the exclusive domain of the sociopolitical sciences.[1] Along with perennially debated issues such as

---

1. For a discussion of this topic, see Johann Baptist Metz, *Faith in History*

trinitarian persons, processions, *perichoresis,* economic-immanent relation, and so on, theologians discuss the trinitarian impact on social issues, and on the trinitarian structures present in human existence and society.[2]

Within the broad range of trinitarian issues there is, as we should expect, a diversity of emphases: Johann Baptist Metz looks at the sociopolitical impact in terms of narrative theology, as he retrieves Ernst Bloch's notion of the "dangerous memory" of Jesus that summons the believer to a more apocalyptic (here-and-now) perspective of social praxis, over a more bourgeois eschatological flow that dilutes social sensibilities and social reform.[3] Karl Rahner and Walter Kasper, through different methodological considerations, look at the Trinity as the (real, tri-personal) manifestation of God's *ad intra* and *ad extra* act of love. Rahner's incarnational emphasis affirms the humanity of Christ as the insuperable act of God's love, as God becomes, in the inexhaustible ocean of divine love, the totally other in the person of Jesus the Christ.[4] Given the contemporary, more rational shift in the concept of person, Rahner offers alternatives to the use of this term to designate the triune reality of God: although reluctant to jettison the word *person* from the trinitarian vocabulary, Rahner feels that, in contemporary philosophical terms, the expressly different (or distinctive) forms of subsistence would be more accurate and intelligible.[5]

Walter Kasper reformulates the traditional "relations of opposition" by focusing on the dimension of such relations as a

---

and Society: Toward a Practical Fundamental Theology (New York: Seabury Press, 1980), 130–32. See also Leonardo Boff, *Trinity and Society* (Maryknoll, N.Y.: Orbis Books, 1988).

2. See note 1 above.

3. Metz, *Faith in History and Society*, 88–99.

4. Karl Rahner, "Theology of Symbol," in *Theological Investigations* IV (New York: Crossroad, 1982), 221–52.

5. Karl Rahner, "Esbozos de una teología de la Trinidad," *Mysterium Salutis* (Madrid: Ediciones Cristiandad, 1977), II/1, 2d ed. 328–31.

dialogue of love eternally spoken between Father, Son, and Holy Spirit. For Kasper, this dialogue finds its foundational reality in the traditional term *perichoresis* already formulated by Gregory of Nazianzus in the fourth century. The interpenetration (without confusion) of the three persons constitutes the theological articulation of this dialogue of love, which supports both diversity and unity, or better yet, the diversity in the unity.[6] Kasper criticizes Rahner's alternative to the term *person* on pastoral grounds: however foreign the original trinitarian use of *person* may be to men and women today, the word may still evoke, from a contemporary homiletic-theological point of view, a relational and dialogical reality that is more pastorally coherent than Rahner's heavily abstract term *forms of subsistence*.[7]

The Relationship of First World and Hispanic Trinitarian Theologies

We have offered our remarks on certain aspects of the trinitarian systems of Rahner, Kasper, and (more briefly) Metz, as representatives of mainstream trinitarian theologies in the First World. Thinkers such as Karl Barth, Gerhard Ebeling, Wolfhart Pannenberg, and others could easily be added. Our purpose, however, is to draw the broader context of First World—or, if the reader wishes, non-Hispanic—trinitarian theologies, as a prolegomenon to our search for the Hispanic profile of God as one and threefold.

A Hispanic theologian who seeks to develop his or her own trinitarian structure must take into account what other contemporary and past trinitarian theologians have said. The Hispanic theologian cannot evade the toil and sweat of scholarly research and reflection. To pretend to replace the required intensity and

6. Walter Kasper, *The God of Jesus Christ* (New York: Crossroad, 1987), 283–85.
7. Ibid, 326–30.

level of scholarship with ill-conceived pseudospiritual or practical theologies would amount to an escapist, nonprofessional theological praxis that would disqualify the Hispanic theologian as a responsible practitioner of the profession.[8] The theologian must command the resources of biblical scholarship, foundational and systematic theology, as well as the ancillary sciences required by the theological enterprise.

The Hispanic theologian retrieves and reformulates into his or her own theological milieu all that he or she sees as true and methodologically sound; the theologian allows First World theological systems to stand critically before his or her system, but he or she also becomes acutely aware that his or her theology must be an even sharper critique of bourgeois and noncommitted theologies that arise from a fatigued, postmodern North-hemispherical Western society.[9]

Furthermore, the Hispanic theologian knows that his or her own methodology has to offer many elements, forgotten or utterly unknown, for the most part, to First World Western colleagues. Although some of these elements (which we will treat further on) are common to all theological latitudes, they all are more intensely lived and reflected upon within the Hispanic religious domain. This applies to Hispanic trinitarian theologies, which constitute the core of this chapter.

The reader will gain a better understanding of our Hispanic trinitarian reflections if we offer some foundations of Hispanic theology in general. We will begin with a brief analysis of fundamental Hispanic theological method. This writer has already offered, in individual and (mostly) joint presentations at recent Catholic Theological Society of America (CTSA) annual meetings, some of these themes in more developed fashion. Here

8. Roberto S. Goizueta, Inaugural Presidential Discourse, Third Annual Meeting of the Academy of Catholic Hispanic Theologians of the United States, 3–5 June 1990, Berkeley, Calif. (unpublished).
9. Metz, *Faith in History and Society*, 88–99.

we will summarize them before we proceed to outline our Hispanic trinitarian theology.

Foundations of Hispanic Theology

In the Domain of Popular Religiosity

In our joint workshop presentations at the Forty-Second and Forty-Third Annual Conventions of the CTSA, as well as in our joint plenary address at the Forty-Fourth Annual Convention, my colleague Orlando Espín and I discussed the structure, sources, and providential-human themes within Hispanic theology.[10] The central concept upon which we built our presentations was popular religiosity. We defined it as

> the set of experiences, beliefs and rituals which more-or-less peripheral human groups create, assume and develop (within concrete socio-cultural and historical contexts, and as a response to these contexts) and which to a greater or lesser degree distance themselves (superficially or substantively) from what is recognized as normative by church and society, striving (through rituals, experiences and beliefs) to find an access to God and salvation which they feel they cannot find in what the church and society present as normative.[11]

We also distinguished between two general Hispanic American religious universes: popular Catholicism, closer to, if not rooted in, mainstream Catholicism; and marginal religions, substantially further from the doctrine, liturgy, and praxis of normative Catholic life.[12]

---

10. Orlando O. Espín and Sixto J. García, "Hispanic American Theology," *Proceedings of the Catholic Theological Society of America* 42 (1987): 114–19; "The Sources of Hispanic Theology," *Proceedings of CTSA* 43 (1988): 122–25; "Lilies of the Field: A Hispanic Theology of Providence and Human Responsibility," *Proceedings of CTSA* 44 (1989): 70–90.
11. Espín and García, "Hispanic American Theology," 115.
12. Ibid.

Popular Religiosity and Hispanic Theology: Reflections on Method

Given the key hermeneutical role of Hispanic popular religiosity, Espín and I developed the theme of "Sources of Hispanic Theology" at the 1988 CTSA convention by analyzing how popular religious tradition deepens and enriches mainstream tradition.[13] I offered a test case for this theory: Hispanic popular passion plays (which will be elaborated on later in this chapter's outline of trinitarian theology). These paraliturgical celebrations unveil (in the Heideggerian sense of the *Enthüllung*—a concept that will surface again in our trinitarian analysis) the implicit Christologies (anti-monophysitic, centered on the salvific, solitary, and very human suffering of Jesus) and ecclesiologies (the entire community participates, rather celebrates the paschal event of Jesus) of the Hispanic faith communities. The same test case proved useful in our plenary address at the 1989 CTSA convention as we developed a Hispanic approach to divine providence and human responsibility.[14]

Popular religiosity conjures the notion of praxis. This term is often associated with the liberation-theological debate on orthopraxis versus orthodoxy.[15] Here we would like to offer some remarks that will again prove useful for our trinitarian theology.

Praxis does not exclude theological reflection (or theoretical/academic theology). One presupposes the other. *Praxis* to the ancient Greeks meant correct practice. This presupposed a reflection on correct and incorrect modes of acting, on good and evil, and so on. The notion of "doing the truth" needs qualification. The truth about a proposition, a system, does not

13. Espín and García, "Sources."
14. Espín and García, "Lilies," 84–86.
15. Leonardo and Clodovis Boff, *Introducing Liberation Theology* (Maryknoll, N.Y.: Orbis Books, 1987), 6–42. See also Leonardo Boff, *Jesus Christ Liberator: A Critical Christology for Our Time* (Maryknoll, N.Y.: Orbis Books, 1979), 43–47.

emerge, as if created out of nothing but praxis itself. This would be a philosophical contradiction in terms. But the explicit reflection of the intuition of a community, responding to that community's popular religious perception of God's salvific action in history, remains open to theological reflection simply because it is rooted in a theological reality and a (often nonthematic) theological response.[16]

My personal reflections offered at a presentation before the CTSA 1990 seminar on trinitarian theology led me to develop my own notion of popular hermeneutics. The popular religious celebration, reflection, belief, and praxis of the community, insofar as they reflect the community's understanding of their relation with God, constitute popular hermeneutics. Through their liturgy, their prayer, their thematic or nonthematic articulations of God, Jesus, Mary, and the church, the community expresses their understanding, their grasp—ultimately, their exegesis—of their faith experience. A celebration such as a passion play, for instance, is nothing less than the popular hermeneutics of the Christ event proper to a given community, that is, the popular understanding and articulation of their Christology.

The Hispanic Theologian as the Thinker, Actor, Poet, and Prophet of the Community

I have already offered thoughts on the Hispanic theologian's commitment to sound theological scholarship. Here I merely add that the preceding reflections on popular religiosity require that the Hispanic theologian correlate these popular religious elements with sound, scholarly biblical, foundational, and systematic reflections. Hispanic theologians, as it were, have the task of providing a language for the faith experience of the community. Here the reader will surely object that this is the

16. Walter Kasper, *Theology and Church* (New York: Crossroad, 1989), 136–37.

SIXTO J. GARCÍA

task of theologians everywhere, that this role is not exclusive to the Hispanic theologian. In principle, such an objection is true. The difference, however, is important: the theologian's interpretive language does not replace the language of the community; it helps deepen the understanding of their faith experience through participatory dialogue with the community. It does not flow from the computer-heavy comfort of First World air-conditioned offices, often peripheral to a community's language, but rather from the living contact with the community's experience.

The preceding considerations underscore the unavoidable commitment of the Hispanic theologian as an acting member of the community. If popular religiosity is a central hermeneutical element for the Hispanic theologian, he or she must be thoroughly involved in the dynamics of the community's popular faith experience. Here I may well apply (with the necessary reformulations and adaptations) Hans-Georg Gadamer's notions of *Zugehörigkeit* ("belongingness.")[17] Gadamer applies this notion to the hermeneutics existent in the language proper to the tradition and heritage of the interpreter. One can easily see how this can be assimilated in terms of the Hispanic theologian's belongingness to the tradition and faith experience of his or her community.

The idea of belongingness finds full meaning within the whole perspective of the oft-mentioned hermeneutical circle (or horizon). The Hispanic theologian functions within the critically and responsibly accepted hermeneutical parameters of his or her community, tradition, and heritage. This acceptance of the hermeneutical context is what allows the theologian to open himself

17. See Richard Palmer's discussion on Gadamer's *Zugehörigkeit* in his *Hermeneutics* (Evanston, Ill.: Northwestern University Press, 1969), 208–9. See also Hans-Georg Gadamer, *Truth and Method* (New York: Crossroad, 1982), 416ff.

or herself, in dialogue and understanding, to other traditions and modes of interpretations.

The idea of the Hispanic theologian as the poet of his or her community may easily evoke the wrong images: a Hispanic theologian as the Walt Whitman, Robert Frost, or Antonio Machado of a community. The notion as such requires explanation.[18] First, theologians and poets have a certain commonality of roles: in their use of language as the bearers of meaning for a community, a social group, a group of theologians or poets, or (more unlikely) to themselves. Second, the language theologians and poets use is never descriptive, never observes a one-to-one correspondence between object and word. Heidegger and Gadamer have reminded us that poets give life to the specific form of being that their verses bear within themselves. We have but to remember Heidegger's dictum in his *Über den Humanismus*: *"Darum ist die Sprache das Haus des Seins und die Behausung des Menschewesens"* ("Language is the house of being and the residence of humanity").[19] The theologian tries to approximate, as Rahner never wearied of repeating, the inexpressible God as Mystery of Love through the ongoing reflection on God's revelation through the prism of the cultural (philosophical, historical) categories of his or her age.[20] He or she theologizes fully aware that his or her language will never capture or define that ineffable God of Love. Not even the sacramental approximation of Jesus of Nazareth can fully unveil him who is Mystery; those

18. See Robert J. Schreiter, *Constructing Local Theologies* (Maryknoll, N.Y.: Orbis Books, 1986), 18–19: "The poet has the task of capturing those symbols and metaphors which best give expression to the experience of a community."

19. Martin Heidegger, *Über den Humanismus*, 8th ed. (Frankfurt am Mein: Vittorio Klosterman, 1981), 51. Originally this was a letter from Heidegger to Jean Beaufret written in the fall of 1946.

20. I owe this definition (with my own modifications) to my dissertation director and dear friend Thomas Franklin O'Meara, Walter K. Warren Professor of Theology at the University of Notre Dame.

who have seen Jesus have seen, definitively but still mysteriously, the Father (John 14:9b).

Both theologian and poet use, often enough, similar language. The theologian relies traditionally on philosophical language, such as analogy of attribution (or proportion), but also resorts to metaphor, symbol, and (occasionally) myth. But are not these different forms of language, on many occasions at least, interwoven with one another? Dave Burrell has argued that all analogy contains metaphor; analogy itself may stand as a symbol for whatever we say of God, since, as Thomas Aquinas has so emphatically affirmed, nothing we predicate of the triune godhead is synonymous with it.[21] The poet also appeals to symbol and myth, to metaphor—and, yes, even to analogy—with the license proper to his trade. In conclusion, we may say that theological language is, in one certain and specific sense, poetic language, even the most dense and difficult to decode. The theologian, hence, is not only the interpreter of the faith experience of a community of which he or she is an active member, but also its poet, who has before him or her unlimited possibilities of liberationist and redemptive creativity.

Is this poetic role, however, exclusive to the Hispanic theologian? It is not—indeed, by definition it cannot be—but it is an indispensable role, a much more intensive role in the Hispanic faith groups than in, say, First World communities. For the Hispanic mind, especially the religious-theological mind, performs in deep contact with myths, stories, traditions, and nature, and this contact, this dialogue, requires a poetic framework in its theological formulations.[22] In expressing the trinitarian concept of *perichoresis*, for example, the Hispanic theologian must formulate it through the analogies of family love, of nature's

21. For the classical discussion on the attributes and the being of God, see Thomas Aquinas, ST Ia, q. 13, a. 3–5.
22. Palmer, *Hermeneutics*, 140.

interpenetration of being, of the metaphors of conjugal inti-
macies, of the beauty of human conversation and dialogue, using
the vocabulary and story frameworks known to and constitutive
of the tradition and heritage of his or her particular community.
Thinker, actor, poet, the Hispanic theologian must also bring
together speculative capacity with a gift for storytelling. His or
her story, after all, is salvation history, with the promise of
healing, integration, and enrichment to the broken Hispanic
world to which he or she belongs.

The Hispanic theologian must be a prophet if he or she is
going to theologize at all. This prophetic element probably will
have become evident to the reader from a reflection on the
preceding roles of the Hispanic theologian. The interpreter, actor, poet-storyteller of a community must unavoidably sing of
the glory of the saving God as well as bewail the injustice,
oppression, and brokenness of the community. His or her theology must point the way to conversion, commitment, involvement with the poorest members of the community, with
the sorrows and frustrations of the people. As an interpreter
and poet who is also a living member of the community, the
Hispanic theologian will probably be one of the oppressed, the
suffering, the maginalized. He or she must share the fate of the
community, lest his or her theology become something foreign
to the experience, especially the faith experience, of the people.
Indeed, the hermeneutical circle or horizon of the Hispanic theologian will be the circle or horizon of those who hope against
all hope, who hunger and thirst, who cringe under the op-
pressing boot, who have only the burning sun or the distant
stars for an abode. The theologian's belongingness will be to a
suffering tradition rooted in hope, to a despised and trampled
people enduring in love. From within this wounded but hope-
filled world, the theological roar of the prophetic lion must be
heard.

Toward a Hispanic Trinitarian Theology

I have devoted the first part of this chapter to the elucidation of the profile, method, and role of Hispanic theologians. I proceed now to attempt the development of a trinitarian theology from the Hispanic theological milieu. I will consider the christocentric dimension of all Hispanic trinitarian formulae, the difficulties in profiling and imaging the Spirit in them, the seminal hermeneutical datum represented by the Marian dimension in Hispanic theology and prayer, and an experiment in articulating the experience of the Trinity in the Hispanic faith communities and societies.

The Christocentric Dimension
of Hispanic Trinitarian Theology

The construction of a Hispanic trinitarian system begins, like any other Hispanic theological project, with the popular religious faith experience of the community. Here I refer again to the practice of passion plays, mentioned in setting our foundational structures.

I have remarked that Hispanic popular Christologies are basically anti-monophysitic (for that matter, anti-docetist). To quote Espín's and my 1989 plenary address, "there are few monophysites in the Hispanic faith communities."[23] The practice and iconography of the passion plays and the Good Friday processions provide the reason why: the bleeding images of Christ bearing the cross or nailed to it, the red-tinted tears flowing from the grief-stricken eyes of the Dolorosa, the mother of sorrows, convey a dimension of very real, and very near, suffering. The broken humanity of Jesus stands as a sacrament of the brokenness of the body of the Hispanic communities. Jesus the Christ is our brother in sorrow and oppression, and we can

23. Espín and García, "Lilies," 84.

touch him, mourn with him, die with him, and yes, also hope with him.

This kenotic Hispanic Christology, however, does not stand in a vacuum. Most passion plays utter the words that Matthew and Mark, drawing from the beginning of Psalm 22, place in the words of Jesus: "My God, my God, why have you forsaken me?" (Mark 15:34; Matt. 27:46). Jesus fulfills God's mysterious but efficacious will of salvation. The Hispanic passion plays reflect, almost universally, this conviction. I remember watching, as a child, the passion play staged by the small and very old parish church about three blocks away from my maternal grandfather's home. As the bleeding icons paraded before the iron gate of my grandfather's front yard, followed by the parish men (chosen from among the tallest and strongest) dressed in imposing Roman legionnaire's garb, wielding what seemed to be very threatening spears, I experienced the slow but certain growth of the sacred all about me. I became totally immersed in the Pasch of the Lord being played out before my eyes. For a few short hours, I lived within sacred space and sacred time, I experienced God's own penetration in time in the person of the suffering Son. Father and Son were there. And the Spirit? It was much later, at an age when theological reflection became possible for me, that I realized that my experience of sacred space and time was the work of the Spirit of holiness and truth, the Spirit who confirms what Jesus had taught, the Spirit sent by the Father through the historic-salvific paschal mystery of the Son. The experience was very real, and it continues to be, in slightly changed fashion, as I celebrate every year the paschal triduum with my community.

The kenotic Jesus symbolizes the presence of God the Father in the communities of faith. The christocentric dimension of Hispanic trinitarian theology utters this reality unequivocally, in celebration, prayer, and belief. There is no Jesus, crucified and risen, without the Father who sent him. But again, what about the Spirit? I have just said how the presence of the Spirit became a reality in my reflection and experience only after I pursued my trinitarian reflections further. What about before the reflective stage? How is the experience of the Spirit, often unthematic, manifested in the praxis of celebration and prayer in the Hispanic communities?

Mary as the Hermeneutical Key to the Trinitarian Experience of the Spirit

The following discussion of the role of the Marian dimension for Hispanic trinitarian theology is not intended to restore an obsolete Marian pietism, as untenable to Catholics as it is to other Christian traditions. I intend to offer theological ruminations on the four-centuries-old reality of the Marian presence in Hispanic faith experience, prayer, and liturgy; most of all, I want to argue how this Marian dimension can help the Hispanic theologian formulate the pneumatological dimension within the context of a Hispanic trinitarian theology. After all, theologians from different Christian traditions agree that the biblical role of Mary as disciple, as hearer of the Word, as the receptor of the Holy Spirit, can offer common points of ecumenical discussion and theologizing.[24]

In his work *Trinity and Society,* Leonardo Boff offers an interesting *theologoumenon.* He argues that the Spirit "pneumatizes" Mary; the Spirit brings about, in the context of God's invitation and Mary's assent in faithful discipleship, the incarnation of the Son, and thereby becomes personified in the person

24. Bertrand Buby, *Mary: The Faithful Disciple* (Mahwah, N.J.: Paulist Press, 1985), 67ff.; André Feuillet, *Jesus and His Mother* (Still River, Mass.: St. Bede Press, 1984), 130ff. For further discussion on the ecumenical dimensions of Mary, see Raymond E. Brown, Karl P. Donfried et al., *Mary in the New Testament* (Philadelphia: Fortress Press—New York; Toronto: Paulist Press, 1978); Frederick M. Jelly, *Madonna: Mary in the Catholic Tradition* (Huntington, Ind.: Our Sunday Visitor, 1986).

of Mary, just as the world took presence (*Shekinah*) in the Tent of the Covenant where the *dabarin* (the words or commandments of the Covenant) were kept. Boff adds that the Spirit became personified in Mary just as the Son became personified in Jesus of Nazareth.[25]

A theologian should dialogue with Boff in this particular text as to his intended meaning. His wording comes close to connoting hypostasis of the Spirit with Mary. Taken in a literal, ontological sense, this would convert Mary into a divine person—indeed, the fourth person of the Trinity. Boff actually uses the word "divinization" to refer to the action and presence of the Holy Spirit in Mary.[26] This expression, however, should not be taken literally, since "divinization" has been used since the age of the Fathers to signify many things: conversion, growth in divine grace, reshaping of the image and likeness of God, and so on. Maximus the Confessor refers to the incarnation and its trinitarian implications as divinizing human beings.[27] It would be somewhat difficult to imagine that such an accomplished theologian as Boff would not advert to the theological (and philosophical) problems resulting from an ontological hypostatization of the Spirit in Mary.

This particular discussion underscores the role of Mary in the Hispanic perception of the unity and trinity in God. It is superfluous to remind the reader of the traditionally seminal role that Mary has played through the centuries in Hispanic prayer and liturgy. This reality springs from an old tradition that associates Mary with the salvific activity of Jesus, and through Jesus with the Father and the Spirit. This Hispanic

25. Boff, *Trinity*, 210–12.
26. Ibid.
27. For a detailed discussion of Maximus's notion of divinization, see Juan Miguel Garrigues, *Maxime le Confesseur: La Charité, avenir divin de l'homme* (Paris: Editions Beauchesne, 1976).

tradition can claim a foundational New Testament background, especially, though not exclusively, in the Gospel of Luke.

Critics in non-Catholic Christian traditions, and also within the Catholic tradition itself, have lamented what they perceive to be pure and simple Mariolatry in the Hispanic communities. While it is undeniable that exaggerations, at least in form and style, have occurred and continue to occur regarding the proper, biblically and theologically founded role of Mary in salvation history and Christian worship, I should like to point out that in most cases this perception of Mariolatry is a misperception. Hispanic faith communities have, as I have said before, a deeply kenotic and incarnational Christology. Jesus is the Son of God, but also a very real and vulnerable human being (indeed, going along with recent discussions by Walter Kasper and William M. Thompson, he is a human person precisely because he is a divine person).[28] He is a member of the Hispanic larger family of saints, indeed the head of the family. The same can be said of Mary: she is unequivocally perceived as the interceding mother, as the ultimate symbol, given to us by God, of feminine strength and loving concern for her own. She is one of us, a creature like us, needing redemption like us, vulnerable to suffering and loneliness like us; and yet, Hispanics see her as the one among us closest to the ineffable mystery of love sacramentalized in Jesus, her son. She is the holiest among us, and that holiness results from the action of the Spirit within her.

In this sense, Boff is right in saying that the Spirit "pneumatizes" Mary and becomes personified in her, for in no other created being has the Spirit acted so decisively and definitively. Within this framework, the Hispanic theologian can discover the clue to the role of the Spirit in a Hispanic trinitarian approach. Hispanic Marian spirituality can become a *locus theologicus* for a

28. Walter Kasper, *Jesús el Cristo*, 6th ed. (Salamanca: Sígueme, 1986), 281ff.; William M. Thompson, *The Jesus Debate* (Mahwah, N.J.: Paulist Press, 1985), 329–33.

theology of the Spirit; Mary becomes the sign of the Spirit of holiness and healing for suffering and marginalized Hispanic faith communities. She points away from herself to the Spirit, who has made her its privileged place of indwelling in salvation history.

The Hispanic theologian can argue that a genuine Hispanic ("economic") trinitarian theology begins with the suffering Son who reflects the mysterious salvific, loving will of the Father, as it points to the Spirit dwelling in the community, of which Mary is the type. From a historico-salvific standpoint, however, the fullness of salvation history begins with Jesus; given this, it could be argued that, from an economic trinitarian standpoint, the Spirit is the beginning of the economic Trinity, since its active, Jesus-begetting dwelling in Mary initiates the Jesus event, which ultimately delivers, through his paschal reality of death and resurrection, a redeemed creation to the Father.

Recently, Virgilio Elizondo has reminded us about the liberating symbol that Mary of Guadalupe has represented for centuries to the Mexicans and Mexican Americans.[29] The story of the epiphany to the Aztec catechumen Juan Diego on the slopes of the Cerro del Tepeyac in 1531 began a process of intimacy in trust and love between the Guadalupana (whose image, imprinted in Juan Diego's *tilma*, crowns the altar of the basilica dedicated to her in Mexico City) and the Mexican people. It is noteworthy to remember, as Deck has pointed out, that as prayer and devotion to Mary of Guadalupe began to spread a short time after Juan Diego reported his encounters, the Spanish clergy tried to root it out from the Mexican Indians they were evangelizing.[30] They regarded it as superstition and

29. Virgilo Elizondo, "Foreword," in Deck, *The Second Wave*, xi–xvi.

30. For an allusion to how the "Morenita del Tepeyac" countered the stratified, programmatic catechesis of the Europeans, see Elizondo, "Foreword," in Deck, *The Second Wave*. The missionary opposition alluded to was mentioned by Elizondo at a 1985 summer theological lectures series at the University of Notre Dame.

pagan syncretism (the epiphanies took place not far from the former shrine of Tonantzín, an Aztec feminine deity); above all, the Spaniards felt threatened by the symbol of hope and redemption that the Guadalupana conveyed for the subdued and oppressed native Mexicans. This hope assumed concrete social and political form in 1810, when the Mexican priest Hidalgo raised the standard of Mexican independence against Spanish colonial rule. At the center of Hidalgo's standard was the image of Mary of Guadalupe.

The Hispanic trinitarian tradition and experience—again, not always thematically expressed—may be described through the (adapted and rethought) concept of unveiling, to which I alluded earlier in this chapter. I have said that one of the roles of the Hispanic theologian is to thematize, to provide, in communal dialogue, the language of the faith experiences, the celebrations, the sufferings, the brokenness, the joys, and the sorrows of his or her community.

I have attempted to show this process of unveiling the trinitarian tradition in Hispanic theology by reflecting on the kenotic Christology of the passion plays and the pneumatological symbol-reality of Mary. The passion plays and the Hispanic emphasis on the kenotic dimension of the Jesus event, as elements of Hispanic popular religious hermeneutics, unveil the particular modes of the presence of Jesus the Christ in the faith communities. In similar fashion, the Marian dimension in prayer, liturgy, and faith-life experience unveils the presence of the Holy Spirit within the same communities.

In personal conversation with this writer, Elizondo criticized Boff's notion of the pneumatization of Mary on the grounds that the people do not conceptualize their relationship with either Mary or the Spirit in such a fashion. The question here, however, is not only how the people explicitly manifest their relationships to God, Jesus, Mary, and the Spirit (that indeed should always be a starting point), but how Hispanic theologians can correlate such popular religious manifestations to the biblical-systematic theological data on the trinitarian God. In the Hispanic communities, the parenthood of God, the redemptive solidarity in suffering of Jesus, and the strong tenderness of Mary are fairly in evidence; the Spirit, however, needs to be unveiled, and this is the task proper to the theologian who reflects on the Hispanic experience.

A Hispanic trinitarian theology must establish the grounds for an experience of the Trinity conceptually accessible to the community, as a necessary complement to the thematically formulated systems and catechesis. For indeed, if the Trinity has entered the economy of salvation, it has become experienceable, and this experience demands from the theologian a language to give it being.

The community experiences God as Father when it recognizes itself as coming from someone or something—specifically, from the loving, creating will of God. When we become aware that we have been sent with a purpose, however dim this awareness may be, we identify ourselves as begotten and sent (not projected or thrown, in the sense of Heidegger's *Entwurf* of being) by God the Father.

When the Hispanic community unveils its identity and thematizes its meaning, even in the midst of oppression and brokenness, and can name this meaning as agape (love), it has experienced the Son as Logos, as Wisdom, as loving redemption.

When the Hispanic community goes a step farther and identifies itself as a living spark of God's love; when it discovers its foundations as love itself; when it experiences that love in self-renewal, in daring to hope for liberation from structures of oppression; when, finally, it interprets its ultimate reality as love sacramentalized in Jesus the Christ, the Son sent by the Father to loosen the unpredictable Spirit of love, healing, and sanctification in the world—then it experiences the Holy Spirit.

Hispanic Trinitarian Theology as a Source of
Liberating and Healing Love

The Trinity as a Unifying Dialogue of Love

Walter Kasper, Leonardo Boff, and others have pointed to the trinitarian structure of creation, history, and society. Boff even proposes looking at the trinitarian profile of social structures, to avoid the ontological, individualistic pitfalls facing those who engage in a discussion of the trinitarian notion of person. Kasper asks whether the sociopolitical impact of trinitarian theology does not constitute the "end of political theology," since a society whose heartbeat echoes the trinitarian dialogue of love has fulfilled the ultimate categories of a theology of the human polis.[31]

These reflections have powerful theological grounds. It is fair to say that Kasper, Boff, Rahner, and others perceive the existential (pastoral, spiritual) impact of trinitarian theology in similar ways, albeit coming from different methodologies: the

trinitarian God is a dynamics of loving dialogue, a *perichoretic* relation comprising the Word, which the Father utters in the Son, which the Son loosens in the world as the Spirit, who in turn constitutes the response in dialogue of God's Word to God. The trinitarian God has, biblically and analogically speaking, an immanent and an economic dimension. Rahner holds for an equation between the two. Kasper fears creeping modalism in Rahner's notion and offers that the biblically and tradition-manifested Mystery of the immanent Trinity finds new (not different!) expression in the theological formulae that speak of the economic Trinity.[32]

The debate surrounding the relation between immanent and economic Trinity, although present in much of what I say in

31. Kasper, *The God of Jesus Christ*, 349.
32. Ibid., 283–85.

this chapter, does not constitute its main point. Suffice to say that this author has suggested to his students possible ways to partially reconcile Rahner's and Kasper's theories. The important concept for our purposes here is the economic-trinitarian dialogue of love that penetrates human history, offering liberation, renewal, hominization. The Trinity thus stamps its profile in every human being's personal reality, and by extension, in every human society and political structure. There is a perichoretic activity in society, in whose structures the trinitarian God images God's self. The original source of this imaging is the trinitarian dialogue of love that grounds the divine oneness in its tri-personality.

The trinitarian image of a God engaged in a salvific dialogue of love with God's self and overflowing into human history provides the Hispanic theologian with a working trinitarian model. The intensely personalistic dimension of Hispanic faith life, as exemplified by its popular celebrations, can identify with a personal God whose tri-personal dialogue empowers human existence with the promise of liberation, redemption from oppression, and inexhaustible love flowing endlessly in the midst of suffering and absurdity.

The Present, Dysfunctional Social Image of the Trinity

Karl Rahner spent a lifetime arguing against hidden or implicit monophysitism, practiced by many sincere and well-meaning Christians. He constantly emphasized, in a number of essays in his *Schriften zur Theologie*, as well as in chapter (or section) 6 of his "little Summa," *Grundkurs des Glaubens* (*Foundations of Christian Faith*), that the humanity of Jesus *is* the humanity of the Son; the sonship of Jesus is constituted by his humanity, and conversely, his humanity is fully affirmed by his sonship lived in full openness and obedience to his Father.[33]

33. Among Rahner's numerous essays and works on the topic: "On the

127

But the humanity of Jesus, sacrament of a healing and redeeming love, has been distorted by social structures that sacrifice human dignity in their polytheistic pantheons, ornamented with the icons of our day: money, power, prestige, racial supremacy, religious intolerance. As Paul VI remarked in *Populorum Progressio* our society is sick.[34] The implicit Christology of our society is, for the most part, comfortably docetic or monophysitic. The privatized Christian experience of the priests of First World consumerism and supremacy divinizes Jesus in order to keep him away from them, at a safe, noninterfering distance; his "dangerous voice" becomes dim, his "dangerous memory" fades away. Society tucks itself safely away from him within the four walls of a building they call "church," as they ignore the larger, dangerous walls of *koinonia* that is the true church, as sacrament of Christ, where there still remain few but powerful prophetic voices demanding justice and redeeming love.

This kind of societal praxis blurs the fundamental notion of incarnation: that in Jesus of Nazareth the Holy Spirit has actualized God's mystery of unfathomable love as a true human being, whose sonship does not distance him from us, but rather brings us, through his filial death and resurrection, renewal and liberation from sin and its sinful personal and social structures. If we allow society to place the incarnate love of God, the human person Jesus of Nazareth, inside the golden cage of undisturbing, bourgeois docetism and monophysitism, then the presence of the creating God, the parental God who wishes to enter our history in the person of Jesus, becomes equally blurred. In the face of this, any language concerning the action and presence of the Holy Spirit becomes a contradiction in terms. Our society

---

Theology of the Incarnation," in *Theological Investigations* IV (New York: Crossroad 1979), 105–25; *Grundkurs des Glaubens: Einführung in den Begriff des Christentums* (Freiburg, Basel, and Vienna: Herder, 1984), 278–98.

34. Paul VI, *Encyclical Letter Populorum Progressio*, nos. 62–67.

defaces, in and through its structures of oppression and sin, the image of the Trinity. The image of the Trinity in society becomes, as it were, dysfunctional.

Most Hispanics in the United States suffer from such a dysfunctional societal image of the Trinity. Many are discriminated against, oppressed, kept in the bondage of inferior educational opportunities, of underpayment, underemployment, and overall marginalization. A Hispanic theology for the United States is not just another idle exercise in sociology of religion. It addresses a vital and urgent problem that will reach crisis levels within a few years. Most recent demographic studies project a growth into the early years of the third millennium that will make Hispanics in the United States the second largest voting group; in terms of Catholicism in this country, Hispanics will become by then the largest single Catholic group within the American church. Yet, if an outsider were to assess the attitude of a large number of American bishops, and an even larger number of European-born or European-descent parish priests, these bare demographic facts, pregnant with consequences for American Catholicism, would hardly be known. Hispanics continue to be, with rare exceptions, marginalized from the American Catholic church.

A Theologically and Socially Functional Image of the Trinity

The Hispanic theologian, among others, has an urgent summons to thematize a functional correlation between immanent/economic theological profiles of the Trinity and its social images. At the risk of sounding repetitious, the Hispanic theologian must turn first to the difficult task of retrieving the true biblical and theological dimension of the incarnation. This implies not so much a dedivinization of Jesus the Christ (avoiding here the discussion of the divinity of Jesus), but rather a true affirmation of his human reality and its implications and demands for a true Christian faith experience.

This retrieval and reformulation of the true face of Jesus Christ presents dangers to our society's conventional wisdom and comfort. This danger is nothing less than that of actualizing God's demand for a renewal of the Covenant, given in personal and communal justice and love. John Meier has argued that the historical Jesus always transcends any attempts to co-opt him as standard for any given ideology; Meier thinks in particular of liberation theology.[35] In our society, however, the danger has an opposite manifestation. Society would love to co-opt Jesus the Christ as the silent, passive guarantor of its greed, selfishness, oppression of the economically weak; they would like this bland, smiling Jesus not to reawaken their dulled sensibilities as they practice racial discrimination, rejection of the destitute migrant, sexism, and the almost infinite number of sins that human creativity, turned demonic, is capable of. Granting the difference in specific cruelties and horrors, as well as in numbers of victims, the broken Hispanic communities may well question, impulsively perhaps, the providence of the God of the *anawim*.

A soundly formulated Christology, however, will reflect the loving face of God. The text of John 14:9b is as true for Hispanic theology as for any other: "Whoever has seen me has seen the Father." Only the face of a Jesus, the Christ of God, who communicates God's transcendental, ultimate victory over the structures of oppression through the paschal pathway of the crushing ignominy of the cross and the radically new humanity of the resurrection, can affirm the permanent presence of God the Father in community.

But this Father-Son relationship, expressed in terms of mission, obedience, death, and resurrection, begins economically, as I have said, with the action of the Spirit, who enters in a personalistic fashion in salvation history through the committed

---

35. John P. Meier, "The Historical Jesus: Rethinking Some Concepts," in *Theological Studies*, 51 (1990): 3–24.

"yes" of Mary; the same Spirit whom Jesus promises as he stands at the threshold of his Pasch (John 14:26; 15:16; 16:13), and who, in a sense, goes back to God the Father bearing a renewed humankind, sacramentalized in the community of forgiveness and the proclamation that it has constituted through the breath of the risen Lord (John 20:19ff.). The Spirit can only sanctify the human polis when the economic fruits of his action, the incarnation and paschal mystery of Jesus, as well as the mission of the church, receive substance, formulation, and experience through theological activity and the experience of the community.

Synthesis of a Hispanic Trinitarian Theology

A Hispanic trinitarian theology must begin with a sound reflection, born of Hispanic popular religious faith experiences and liturgies, on Christology, in particular the kenotic and paschal dimensions of Jesus the Christ.

This kenotic approach, however, cannot ignore the best theological insights into the incarnation. A docetist or monophysitic Jesus offers neither healing nor liberation. This is true, of course, of all responsible christological systems, Hispanic and otherwise. It bears, however, a special meaning in Hispanic communities, where the true humanity of Jesus, the victim of suffering, discrimination, rejection, and oppression, is essential to the whole of the communities' faith life.

The Hispanic theologian ought to emphasize the resurrection as the proleptic liberation from structures of oppression and the actualization of the new human being, the new creation, the dawn of the (never complete, but very much in progress) new age of justice and love for Hispanic groups within the ecclesial community and the political society.

The Marian dimension remains the privileged locus for the Hispanic theologian out of which the pneumatological dimension of his or her trinitarian system emerges. Mary becomes the symbol of the personal indwelling of the Holy Spirit among humankind, as she points away from herself to the action of the Spirit who brings the fullness of the Father's love into this, our broken society, through the sacrament of Jesus' true humanity, the true (and never separable) humanity *of the Son.*

A Hispanic trinitarian theology, therefore, follows the initial economic action of the Spirit, dwelling in the person of Mary, actualizing the salvific humanity of Jesus of Nazareth, Son and Christ of God, obedient to this God whom he calls "Abba." This is the same Son whose death and resurrection usher in the new eon of salvation, healing, and renewal, as he releases and sends the Holy Spirit, his own Spirit and the Father's, into the structures of a sinful and dehumanized society. There, the de-faced, socially docetic image of the nonexistent, harmless Christ will be changed radically, and then society will see the true face of God in the true Jesus, borne by the Spirit, as he utters, or better yet, cries out the message of justice, of self-sacrifice, of unconditional love, of common good over privatized greed, of a common working bench over consumerism, of an attitude of awe and wonder before the irreducible dignity of all men and women, over discrimination and racism. This, and no less, must be the fundamental structure and outline of a Hispanic trinitarian theology.

6

Grace and Humanness:
A Hispanic Perspective

Orlando O. Espín

The grace of God, in Christian theology, is a subject—or, I should say, an experience—of utmost importance. Christianity is not understandable without what we call grace. Few battles in Christian history have been so fierce as those fought over grace. And few theological topics have provoked so much literature and engaged so many brilliant minds as has grace throughout the centuries.[1]

My purpose is to point briefly to the relationship between grace and humanness, and to reflect theologically on some possible significance of this relationship for U.S. Hispanics.[2]

1. For a brief history of the theology of grace, see P. Fransen, "Desarrollo histórico de la doctrina de la gracia," in *Mysterium Salutis* ed. J. Feiner and M. Löhrer, (Madrid: Ediciones Cristiandad, 1969), IV/2, 611–730.
2. The term *Hispanic*, in this chapter, refers not to a single ethnic or cultural group (such as Mexican Americans, Puerto Ricans, or Cuban Americans), but to what in fact is a community of communities, each with its distinct history and culture, but united by some fundamental elements such as worldview, language, family structures, and religion. Popular religiosity, even with its many variations, is one of the most powerful, typical, and commonplace links that bind all U.S. Hispanic communities. The origins of

It is important to set forth the background and limits of this discussion. First of all, I am Roman Catholic. This means, among other things, that I am a member of a Christian tradition that values community and symbol and views the communal and sacramental dimensions of Christianity as necessary. This also means that, when speaking of grace, I regard humanness as a worthy locus of God's activity and human response. And third, as a Catholic I reflect on grace as a member of a very long theological tradition that allows for ample diversity. These three elements will be apparent throughout this chapter.

Besides being Catholic, I am also Hispanic. I will contend here that culture is a necessary prism through which we perceive God's grace and through which we respond to it. Therefore, to be Hispanic for me is not superficial, an accident of birth, but rather is the very condition within and through which I can hear the gospel and respond to it in faith. And what I am saying of myself is equally true of every U.S. Hispanic. Those of us who are Catholic are not just Catholics who happen to be Hispanic— we are Catholic in a Hispanic way, and we cannot be in any other way. Our Hispanic culture thus makes us experience the grace of God in a specific fashion, a way that would not be available to us were we not Hispanic. As a consequence, the theological reflection presented in this chapter must be understood within the context of Hispanic culture, experience, and reality.

I must also say something about what has begun to be called U.S. Hispanic theology.[3] This theology, in my view, is not

---

all of these communities can be traced back to the Spanish colonial period in both Latin America and the United States, and to the particular phenomenon called *mestizaje*, whereby either native populations or African slaves racially and culturally mixed with the Spanish element to form what today are the diverse U.S. Hispanic communities. Finally, the term *Hispanic* refers not to Latin America but to the ethnic and cultural groups here described in the United States.

3. Much is being written from a Hispanic theological perspective. As

defined merely by the fact that its authors might be culturally Hispanic. Nor do I believe that what makes a theology Hispanic is the topics it deals with or its heavy use of Hispanic symbols or catch phrases. It seems to me that what makes a theology Hispanic is its source and its method. All subjects of theology, including grace, are open to it; but the sources of the reflection and the way the subject is methodologically approached, are the keys to a distinctly "Hispanic" theology.

These clarifications are necessary because this chapter is written from a Catholic perspective and, specifically, from a Hispanic one. It deals with the theology of grace and, methodologically, it springs solely from reflection on the Hispanic Catholic experience of individuals and communities in which I have had the privilege to serve and work. Because it deals with grace and humanness, it will probably not speak to Hispanics only.

I will attempt to present a view of grace that is coherent with Scripture and, specifically, sprung from our Hispanic communities' sense of God and of humanness. For this purpose I will first discuss the God of grace and then what it means to be human as an image of this God. I will then examine the processes of humanization and dehumanization, as these reflect the paths toward the fullness of what we are or toward the derailment of our foundational calling.

I will continue with a review of the role of culture and of its relationship to grace, emphasizing Hispanic culture. Within this context, I will examine popular religiosity as a privileged locus for Hispanic self-disclosure. Popular religiosity will help

---

examples, see: Espín and García, "Hispanic American Theology," 114–19; "Sources," 122-25; and "Lilies of the Field," 70–90. See also Isasi-Díaz and Tarango, *Hispanic Women*; Elizondo, *Christianity and Culture*; Elizondo, *Galilean Journey;* Elizondo, *The Future Is Mestizo;* Deck, *The Second Wave.* The founding in 1988 of the Academy of Catholic Hispanic Theologians of the United States brought together, for the first time, the vast majority of Catholic theologians writing and teaching from a Hispanic perspective. The academy's mission includes the promotion of a distinctively United States Hispanic theology.

us discover values and experiences that are essential in any reflection on grace. But Hispanic popular religiosity is lacking in some equally important areas, thus requiring that we go beyond it to conclude a study on the action of God's grace.

I realize that I intend to cover much, and I am also aware that I have a limited format within which to accomplish it. So some themes will merely be indicated and others will be briefly touched upon. My intention, as stated at the very beginning, is only to point to the relationship between grace and humanness and to reflect theologically on a possible significance of that relationship for Hispanics.

The God of Grace

To speak of grace means, necessarily, that we speak of God. But what God are we referring to? The history of Christian thought is witness to how the numerous understandings of God have shaped theological controversies and developments.[4]

It is impossible for us to review here twenty centuries of reflection on the subject. It is also impossible to adequately discuss here the role that human language, experience, and symbol play in all God-talk.

God, as understood here, is the God who is love—not a God who simply acts with love, displays love, is moved to love, and so on, no matter how outstanding and extraordinary that love might be. Rather, the God I am referring to is the God who *is* love. The very essence of divinity is love and, as a consequence, there is nothing God can be or do that is not loving. There is nothing God can be or do that is not expressive of that love

---

4. See, for example: D. Nichols, *Deity and Domination* (London: Routledge, 1989); J. A. Ruiz de Gopegui, *Conhecimento de Deus e evangelização* (São Paulo: Loyola, 1977); J. P. Miranda, *Marx y la Biblia* (Mexico: CRT, 1970); R. Muñoz, *Dios de los cristianos* (Madrid: Paulinas, 1987); F. Houtart, *Religion et modes de production précapitalistes* (Brussels: Editions de l'Université de Bruxelles, 1980).

which God is. And nothing God can do or be could ever contradict, or be exempt from, divine love. God is love and nothing else.[5]

This God who is love is so in a divine manner. In other words, God is love without limits, without exceptions, without conditions, and eternally. If this is true, then all divine attributes can only be attributes of divine love, because they are attributes of the divine being. Thus, for example, God's omnipotence is not raw might, an expression of unbounded macho power. Rather, God's omnipotence is that might that is possible only through limitless, eternal love. That's why the cross can be called a mighty act of God.[6]

The God of Christians is a trinitarian God, the one who, forever remaining one, is also an eternal community of love. In other words, the internal and eternal reality of God is expressive of the love that God is. That which binds and is the oneness of the Trinity is the love that the Three share and are among themselves.

This God who is love, freely choosing to be authentically and fully that which God is, called another into existence, not as a sign of capriciousness, and not as expressive of raw might, but as a freely chosen consequence of that love which God is. Creation exists as the first sacrament of God's love and life, and as the first other that God loves. It is in the ongoing act of creation that we first detect that which can be called grace— God's loving self given to us and for us as an expression of that which God is. God-for-us is grace.

---

5. Compare 1 John 4:16-17, Isa. 49:13-16, Luke 15:1-32. See also R. Schnackenburg, *Cartas de Juan* (Barcelona: Herder, 1980), 256–64; S. S. Smalley, *1,2,3 John*, Word Biblical Commentary, vol. 51 (Waco: Word Books, 1984), 49, 61.
6. Compare 1 Cor. 1:20b-25.

Humanity as "Graced" Image of God

In the process of ongoing creation humanity came to be not as mere accident but as willed. Scripture,[7] in witnessing to the divine motive for creating human beings, teaches that God meant humanity to be the divine image. In view of the Hebrew abhorrence of all images of God, the claim that humans are *the* image of God is an extremely powerful statement.

At the most profound level, to be human is to be an image of God. It is God, therefore, who is the source and ultimate definition of humanness. And the God whose image we are is the God who is love.

Therefore, to be human is not just to exist knowing that we ultimately come from God. Rather, to be human is to *be* the image of love, of an eternally communitarian (that is, trinitarian) God. And, as a consequence, one cannot claim to be truly human unless one is loving, and not just loving in an individual way but also in a communitarian way (given the trinitarian reality of God).

Our being the image of God also implies that our humanness was created out of love and solely for the purpose of loving. We have the very being of God inscribed in our own being, to the point that we cannot understand ourselves apart from this imprint. Paraphrasing Karl Rahner, it can be said that human beings are that which God is when God expresses God's self outside of the sphere of the divine.[8] And if it is true that God is love, then that understanding of humanness is extremely important.

To be the image of God is a gift from God. We did not merit it and could do absolutely nothing to achieve it. We are gifts.

7. Gen. 1:26.
8. See Karl Rahner, "Concepción teológica del hombre," ed. Rahner et al., *Sacramentum Mundi* (Barcelona: Herder, 1976), III, 493–504; Rahner, *Foundations of Christian Faith* (New York: Crossroad, 1985), 26–42, 75–81, 117–33.

God's pouring of God's loving life created us, without our having deserved it, and for the sole purpose of loving us. Our very being is graced. Because of this, all human beings can look at themselves, by the mere fact that they are images of God, as graced.[9] No human being, I believe, has ever been without this foundational grace. Otherwise we would have to claim that some human beings are not images of God, that some do not find their ultimate definition and reality in the God of love who created them.

Humanity as Historical and as Sinful

Humans are historical beings. It is a constitutive dimension of ourselves that we grow, that we learn, that we become. Although from the beginning we are human, we also *become* human as we live our lives in history, both individually and communally. The historical processes whereby we become more fully human we can call humanization. Given all that has been said above, it can be affirmed that the most profound and ultimate goal of authentic humanization is our becoming more fully that which we are—images of the trinitarian God of love.

It is unnecessary to repeat that in order to more fully humanize ourselves we must love. It is also needless to say that our human freedom, a necessary condition for loving, has not always chosen authentic humanization. Rather, humans can and do choose to derail their foundational vocation to humanness, in a vain attempt to redefine themselves in manners that exclude or manipulate the God who is the source of all that is truly human. The processes whereby human beings derail themselves

9. See Karl Rahner, "Gracia: exposición teológica," in *Sacramentum Mundi*, III, 319–34. See also M. Gelabert Ballester, *Salvación como humanización: Esbozo de una teología de la gracia* (Madrid: Paulinas, 1985); M. de França Miranda, *Libertados para a práxis da justiça: A teología da graça no atual contexto latino-americano* (São Paulo: Loyola, 1980).

from their ultimate goal we can call dehumanization. It is apparent that dehumanization is also what traditional Christian terminology has called sin.

My use of the verb derail in this context is due to the Hebrew notion that sin is "missing the mark"; it is the derailment of what should be.[10] If the ultimate goal for us is our becoming more fully the human images of God, then any attempt to move away from that goal is to "miss the mark," to sin, to dehumanize ourselves, and will in the end lead to perdition, to being lost. Sin, in the last analysis, is an extremely irresponsible attempt to become that which we are not. Sin is a murderous attempt against our very being. Needless to say, it is doomed to painful failure because sin could never overcome the God of love.

Nevertheless, we humans seem to be all too frequently engaged in the mad quest to redefine ourselves by excluding God and God's fundamental definition of our beings. We continue in our attempt to become human without love and without being images of love. As I said, our attempts are doomed to failure—as history shows, often very costly failure. As dehumanization has become part of our reality, it has prevented and will continue to prevent the success of all our efforts to remedy our sinful condition and its consequences. At the sight of history one can understand how, from the beginning, Christian tradition has insisted that we humans cannot save ourselves and heal the loving relationship that is at the very core of our being.[11]

Earlier I stated that all humans, regardless of their dehumanization, are graced because they remain ultimately human. This means that sin can never blot out the image of God within

10. See R. Knierim, "Errar, pecar," in E. Jenni and C. Westermann, eds., *Diccionario teológico manual del Antiguo Testamento* (Madrid: Cristiandad, 1978), I, 755–65.
11. See, for example, P. Schoonenberg, "El hombre en pecado," in *Mysterium Salutis*, II, 654–725; de França Miranda, *Libertados para a práxis da justiça*, 59–78.

us. It also means that the love of God and the God of love are not held hostage by human sinfulness. God is God, and God's divinity (which we have imaged as love) is not dependent in any way on humanity's actions. God's love for us, therefore, is not diminished or ended because of our refusal to correspond.

If it is true that God is love, and that God's love continues regardless of humanity's condition, then the outpouring of God's love—which is the only way God can authentically be—must also continue. In history this also means that God would go on offering God's loving self to us in concrete, specific, perceivable ways.[12] People of faith do attest to that throughout the centuries. However, Christians claim that the definitive, irrevocable outpouring of God's loving self in history occurred in the person, ministry, death, and resurrection of Jesus of Nazareth.[13] God not only loved us in Jesus, but gave God's self to us in that outstanding manner we have traditionally called incarnation.

As if to break the boundaries of what we thought possible for God's love, this love gave the incarnate Son—the visible image of the invisible God—into the hands of the human creature, not for the purpose of crucifixion (that would imply divine masochism), but as the ultimate and definitive outpouring of God's loving self to us. Crucifixion is the consequence of human sinfulness, and the willful acceptance of it is the result of divine love. The being of God is seen on the cross. The might of God, as the boundless power of love, is expressed on the cross. The love of God, and the true nature of all love that images God's, is willing to take all risks (even the risk of rejection and death) for the beloved. Crucifixion is not the purpose of the incarnation—the love of us is. Crucifixion is our response to that love.[14]

12. See L. Boff, *Gracia y liberación del hombre* (Madrid: Cristiandad, 1978), 53–147.

13. See John 3:34, 7:17-18, 14:6-14; Acts 2:22-36; 2 Cor. 4:1-6; Col. 1:15; Rom. 8:37-39; Heb. 1:1-12. See also E. Schillebeeckx, *Jesus: An Experiment in Christology* (New York: Crossroad, 1981), 636-74.

14. See Karl Rahner, "Encarnación," in *Sacramentum Mundi*, II, 549-66.

Resurrection is God's last, irrevocable word to us. No matter how dehumanized we might have become, no matter how sinful, the love of God is forever pledged to us in the resurrection of the Son. Sin has not and will never overcome God's authenticity, God's love for us. Sin can never blot out from us the fundamental definition and most radical level of our being as the beloved of God, as the images of divine love.[15]

But, as can be deduced from the above, we humans have done nothing to merit all this love. We have done and can do nothing to force God's outpouring to us. We did nothing to make incarnation happen; we did nothing to make God willfully accept crucifixion; we did nothing to bring about the resurrection. Our unhappy contribution was the crucifixion. The love of God, and the historical outpouring of that love that was Jesus of Nazareth, have been given to us in utter freedom, with no other explanation than the limitless love of God.[16]

Our salvation, therefore, is a wonderful by-product of the love of God shown in the incarnation and death and resurrection of the Son. We are saved because we are loved. We are *not* saved because God had to figure out a way of fixing the world we had messed up. To respond to Jesus as the definitive word of God to us, is to put ourselves on the road to humanization; it is to start becoming what we were and are from the beginning.[17] It is to believe that we can be what God made us to be, not because we have discovered a human-made formula, but because we have discovered the love of God shown to us in and through Jesus, and because that discovery now allows us to act accordingly.

The outpouring of God's love in and through Jesus, and our discovery and response to it, all happen in history—and if in history, then also in culture, because no human, historical being

15. See Gelabert Ballester, *La salvación como humanización*, 144–54.
16. See, for example, John 3:16; Eph. 1:4-12, 2:4-10.
17. Ballester, *La salvación como humanización*, 154–58.

is ever outside of culture. Here is where the theology of grace gets complicated, because it is humanly impossible to perceive, understand, and respond to God's love in ways that are not cultural. God is not bound to human culture, but human beings are, and there is no possibility of this being otherwise.

The Role of Culture

Culture can be briefly described as the dynamic sum of all that a human group does and materially and symbolically creates in order to prolong its life in history within geographical contexts. It is culture that allows any human group, and its individual members, to discover meaning and act accordingly. Society and culture dialectically create and modify each other.[18]

This description of culture would seem to imply many things. Among others, and as just mentioned, no human society and no human individual can even dream of the possibility of existing without culture. That dream itself would be a cultural exercise, made possible precisely by the culture of the dreamer. We are in culture as in a womb from which there is no birth, because we are already born into it.

Obviously, cultures are not impermeable. They do change, grow, and die. But in the very long history of culture, individuals and communities never explain or view themselves except

18. The literature on culture, its meaning and definition, is vast. As suggestive examples, see R. A. Shweder and R. A. LeVine, eds., *Culture Theory* (London: Cambridge University Press, 1984); P. L. Berger and T. Luckmann, *The Social Construction of Reality* (New York: Doubleday, 1966); C. Geertz, *The Interpretation of Cultures* (New York: Basic Books, 1973); R. A. LeVine, *Culture, Behavior and Personality* (Chicago: Aldine, 1973); V. W. Turner, *The Forest of Symbols* (Ithaca, N.Y.: Cornell University Press, 1967); R. W. Casson, *Language, Culture and Cognition* (New York: Macmillan, 1981); E. T. Hall, *The Silent Language* (New York: Doubleday/Anchor, 1973). For a fuller bibliography, see Orlando O. Espín, "Inculturación de la fe: planteamiento del problema teológico-pastoral," in *Estudios Sociales* 62 (1985): 1–31.

through the tools of understanding granted them by culture. These tools, as I call them, place certain limits on what can be affirmed as real, as good, as true, as beautiful, as possible. Although facilitating understanding, these tools also limit it to what is culturally possible.

The church, formed by individuals and communities of the most diverse cultural backgrounds, is no exception to this rule of culture.[19] It would be nonsense to pretend that the cultures of its members have not affected the ways in which the church has understood the gospel and reflected upon it throughout the centuries. Besides being anthropological nonsense, this pretension would imply a denial of what is meant by the incarnation.

Christ lived in a specific time period, in a specific land, within a concrete history, and within a single culture. Jesus of Nazareth was a first-century, Palestinian Jew, and there is no way to responsibly understand him by disregarding these historical, geographical, and cultural facts. Modern biblical exegesis has more than sufficiently shown this to be true.

And, after Jesus, all Christians have also lived in historical, geographical, and (especially) cultural milieux. All Christian preaching and sacramental celebrations, all Christian witnessing and living, all Christian theologizing and doctrinal statements, and all shapes of the church throughout history, have occurred within specific cultural contexts that have, of necessity, acted as occasions and tools for Christian understanding, doctrine, life, and decision making. Nothing human in Christianity is acultural. Nothing! Only that which is unlimited by culture in the

19. See, for example, Espín, "Inculturación de la fe"; L. J. Luzbetak, *The Church and Cultures* (Maryknoll, N.Y.: Orbis Books, 1988); P. Schineller, *A Handbook on Inculturation* (New York: Paulist Press, 1990); A. J. Gittins, *Gifts and Strangers* (Mahwah, N.J.: Paulist Press, 1989); A. Shorter, *Toward a Theology of Inculturation* (Maryknoll, N.Y.: Orbis Books, 1988); C. Geffré, *Le christianisme au risque de l'interprétation: Essais d'herméneutique théologique* (Paris: Editions du Cerf, 1983).

church we also find unlimited by Christ's humanness: the God of love and the love of God. This is why the Christian message, which is ultimately the message of God, can be preached, believed, and lived in any human culture: being God's, it transcends all cultures.

However, the ones who preach, believe, and live the gospel are human beings, and though the source of the gospel is not limited to culture, Christian human beings are. Therefore, their way of being Christian (and of understanding the reasons for it and the consequences of it) will be necessarily cultural. This implies many things, but for our purposes here, this centrality of culture means that the way individuals and communities humanize or dehumanize themselves will be cultural. The role of culture also means for Christianity that the way a people or a person experientially perceives the love of God, and the way they respond to it, will always be cultural. In other words, there is no acultural Christianity, just as there is no acultural option for God, love, and salvation.

Therefore, if to be human is to be an image of God, and if to be an image of God is to be foundationally graced, then this is also a cultural reality, because no one can be truly human outside of culture. But just as humans can dehumanize themselves, so can cultures bear the sinful imprint of the humans that create them. All cultures are also dehumanized and dehumanizing, and in need of the liberating love of God. All cultures need salvation. As a consequence, no culture can ever claim to be—of itself, and in comparison with other cultures—better suited to incarnate the Christian message.

Grace and Culture

Grace as it is in itself (that is, God's eternal, inner self as love) is not bound by culture. But grace as it is for and within us (which is the only grace we can experience) shows itself as cultural because *we* are cultural.

Traditional Catholic theology used to speak of grace as being uncreated *and* created.[20] In other words, grace, as it is God's eternal, inner self as love, is evidently uncreated. And grace, viewed as God's gift of God's self to humankind and as God's actions in, for, and within us, though uncreated in its source, is nevertheless created insofar as this self-giving and these actions of God do occur in history and not eternally. Perhaps we might not feel comfortable with traditional theological categories and terminology, but there are certain intuitions behind the created/ uncreated distinction that I find useful and valid.

Both of these categories (created and uncreated) define grace as the way God is, one in God's eternal self and the other as God is for us. In other words, this traditional view is clearly implying that God is love, freely giving God's self within the eternal trinitarian relation and outwardly to the creatures. The Trinity is certainly beyond all time and limit. But not so the human creature. If God as grace-in-itself is eternally transcending history and culture, God as grace-for-and-within-us would be utterly meaningless and beyond our perception unless that grace entered our creaturely world, worked through and within our history and our cultures, and molded itself to our (cultural!) understanding, making it possible for us to see and touch the gracious actions of the God-who-is-for-us.[21] Given the historical, changing character of our cultures, these actions of God for us must in turn be changing, adapting, and molding themselves to our diversity. Thus, what can truthfully be called a graced moment or action in one place or at one time or for one group in human history might not be considered truthfully graced for another. Perhaps it could even be perceived as disgrace in another context.

20. See, for example, C. Baumgaertner, *La gracia de Cristo* (Barcelona: Herder, 1982), 118–21; P. Fransen, "Desarrollo histórico de la doctrina de la gracia," 638–56.
21. See Boff, *Gracia y liberación*, 53–147, 221–36.

If the ultimate will of God for us is that we become that which we are from creation (that is, truly human, images of the God who is love), then this divine will must include our cultural dimension, since we cannot be human without culture. Or put another way, it must be the will of God that each of us humanize him or herself in the manner in which we are human, and that manner is specifically cultural. To trample on the culture of a human group, therefore, cannot be justified in the name of the Christian God, because it would imply a denial of the incarnation of grace. Furthermore, it would reject the possibility that the trampled-on human group might have of perceiving and responding to the love of the God-for-them.

Grace and Hispanic Culture

If the basic arguments presented in this chapter are so far correct, then it is reasonable to state that the experience of grace possible to U.S. Hispanics, in order to be authentically an experience of the God-for-us, must be culturally Hispanic. Deculturization, in the name of Christianity, would be dehumanizing and (as a consequence) sinful. To trample on Hispanic culture while pretending to evangelize is to impede the very experience of the God that saves, because, as we have seen, the experience of grace can only be had in and through one's culture. To dehumanize, as we discussed earlier, is to actively oppose the God of love and salvation, and to deculturalize or to trample on culture is dehumanizing.

The other side of this argument is the implied belief that non-Hispanic culture (in our American context, Anglo culture) is either part of the gospel message or the superior vehicle for its expression. That belief is not only utter nonsense but outright evil.

All of this having been said, a question arises that must be dealt with. How does a Hispanic individual or community encounter the God-for-us (in other words, experience grace) in a culturally authentic way? Perhaps it is easier to say how it should not be done. But we must attempt to address this question and search for answers, even if no totally satisfactory ones are to be found.

Popular Religiosity as Locus of Hispanic Self-disclosure

It has always been my contention that popular religiosity is a privileged vehicle for Hispanic cultures.[22] Popular religiosity has been, and still is, the least "invaded" cultural creation of our peoples, and a locus for our most authentic self-disclosure. It is through popular religiosity that we have been able to develop, preserve, and communicate deeply held religious beliefs. Through it we experience profound encounters with God. While popular religiosity is not the only means for the development and preservation of our cultures, it would be extremely difficult (if not impossible) to think about or understand Hispanic cultures without finding the crucial role that popular religiosity has played (and still plays) in our midst as matrix and vehicle of our most authentic values and selves.[23]

Hispanic popular religiosity is a parallel complex of symbols, rites, experiences, and beliefs that our peoples, feeling themselves marginalized from the mainstream of society and church, have developed and sustained in order to communicate with God and experience salvation.[24] Much can and should be said

22. See Orlando O. Espín, "Religiosidad popular: un aporte para su definición y hermenéutica," *Estudios Sociales* 58 (1984): 41–56; *Evangelización y religiones negras* (Rio de Janeiro: PUC, 1984); "Hacia una teología de Palma Sola," Estudios Sociales 50 (1980): 53–68; and Espín and García, "Hispanic American Theology," "The Sources of Hispanic Theology," and "Lilies of the Field."

23. See Elizondo, *Christianity and Culture*, 174–94; Deck, *The Second Wave*, 113–25; D. T. Abalos, *Latinos in the United States: The Sacred and the Political* (Notre Dame, Ind.: University of Notre Dame Press, 1986), 106–39.

24. The literature on popular religiosity is vast and growing. As examples,

about this brief definition of popular religiosity, but our format here does not allow a detailed discussion of this fascinating and important subject.

Popular religiosity, as I said, is a privileged locus of Hispanic self-disclosure and culture. Through it we say that we experience the life of society and church from the margins. We say, however, we are capable of creating and sustaining alternatives. We have not yielded to hopelessness, but rather continue to believe and search for a way out of our marginal status. Somehow we suspect that what is presented to us as normative by society and church is not fully so.

Hispanics have created their parallel ways to God, to life, and to salvation. Evidently, most Hispanics do not consciously think of their popular religiosity in these terms. But a close,

see P. H. Vrijhof and J. Waardenburg, eds., *Official and Popular Religion: Analysis of a Theme for Religious Studies* (The Hague: Mouton, 1979); S. Galilea, *Religiosidad popular y pastoral* (Madrid: Cristiandad, 1979); P. A. Ribeiro de Oliveira, *A religião do povo* (Curitiba, Brazil: Cadernos Universidade Católica, 1976); V. Turner and E. Turner, *Image and Pilgrimage in Christian Culture* (New York: Columbia University Press, 1978); F. C. Rolim, *Religião e classes populares* (Petrópolis, Brazil: Vozes, 1980); L. Maldonado, *Introducción a la religiosidad popular* (Santander, Spain: Sal Terrae, 1985); L. Maldonado, *Génesis del catolicismo popular* (Madrid: Cristiandad, 1979); A. Cabré Ruffat, ed., *La fe de un pueblo: Historia y misión* (Santiago, Chile: Mundo, 1977); J. A. Estrada, *La transformación de la religiosidad popular* (Salamanca: Sígueme, 1986); J. Vidal, "Popular Religion among Hispanics in the General Area of the Archdiocese of Newark," in *Presencia Nueva: A Study of Hispanics in the Archdiocese of Newark* (Newark: Archdiocesan Office of Research and Planning, 1988), 235–352. See also the bibliography in note 22. For more complete bibliographies, see *Conferência Nacional dos Bispos do Brasil: Bibliografia sobre religiosidade popular* (São Paulo: Paulinas, 1981. Estudos da CNBB, vol. 27); C. Johansson and I. Pérez, "Bibliografía sobre religiosidad popular," *Teología y vida*, 28/1–2 (1987): 105–73. See also the yearly listings and commentaries, on recent literature dealing with popular religiosity, in the excellent *Bibliografía teológica comentada del área iberoamericana*, published annually by ISEDET, Buenos Aires. Some fundamental church texts on the subject are the Puebla Document, nn. 444–69, 910–15, 959–63; the Medellín Conclusions, 6:2–5, 8:2; and Paul VI's *Evangelii Nuntiandi*, nn. 48, 63.

detailed study will show how the motifs of alternative, parallel means, of hope against the odds, of quiet rebellion against marginalization, and of doubt as to the absolute validity of that which pretends to be the normative, are all implicitly present and operative in popular religiosity. Rigorous study will also discover a deeply felt and held faith in the goodness of God and in the ultimate triumph of what is fair and just.[25]

The means by which popular religiosity grasps and conveys these motifs are "popular," and by this I do not merely mean that they are widespread. They are indeed. But these means are popular mainly because they literally come from the people themselves. It is often hard to discover the historical specifics of when a given symbol began to be used, or a specific rite began to be practiced, or a belief to be held. Popular religiosity today is the result of the anonymous contributions of many generations. These contributions are expressed through the symbols, rites, and beliefs that were and are culturally possible or available to people, substantially or peripherally modified in order to convey whatever experiences or motifs need to be communicated at the time. Since the symbols, rites, and beliefs of church and society are perceived as (at the very least) unsatisfactory or inadequate, Hispanics will create their own or improve on those already available.

But although Hispanic popular religiosity does contain and express a great deal of goodness, of faith, and of trust, it is also evident that it has within it the wounds of the very marginalization it quietly wants to rebel against. This cultural creation of our people conveys the reality of Hispanics. The courage and the fear, the hope and the fatalism, the faith in God and the temptation to magical manipulation, the strength of the family and the machismo of our patriarchal society, the deep respect for motherhood and the stereotyping of women—all this and much more are to be found in Hispanic popular religiosity.

25. See Espín, "Religiosidad popular," 44–47.

To admit these strengths and wounds is to acknowledge that Hispanic popular religiosity is a reflection of our reality and of our culture. And our reality, by and large, is difficult. The poverty and marginalization of the majority of U.S. Hispanics, together with their accomplishments, faith, courage, and hope, are all present in popular religiosity. We create popular religiosity, and in turn it certainly shows what and who we are.

I said earlier that no culture is fully humanizing. This applies to Hispanic cultures as well, and popular religiosity, as a key cultural component, is a witness to it. Our many Hispanic cultures show themselves to be wounded by dehumanization, by sin (both the sin of our people and the sin of those who marginalize us). Hispanic cultures—including popular religiosity as one of their main building blocks—are also in need of the saving favor of God, though this favor never shows itself in ways that are culturally incomprehensible to us.

Long is the list of Hispanic accomplishments and contributions, though the dominant Anglo ideology would rather have us ignore the facts and continue to believe in some pretended innate Hispanic inferiority. Popular religiosity, as a privileged locus of our self-disclosure, self-understanding, and culture, has introjected some of the virus of this ideology, but somehow it has also managed to create mechanisms for the rejection of this virus. A close observation of the complex elements that form the popular religious universe will show that Hispanics do not believe themselves to be hopelessly in bondage. If there is a strong thread binding all the elements of popular religiosity together, it is the deep hope that life and the world *can* change. I will readily grant that some of the means employed to promote that change are often symbolic and sometimes outright magical, but this does not cancel at all the fundamental drive, the hope in the possibility of change![26]

26. See Espín, *Evangelización y religiones negras*.

It is this drive, this hope, that implicitly makes popular religiosity a force (albeit symbolic) against poverty, marginalization, and the dominant ideology. Hispanic popular religiosity is a daily reminder that things need not be as they are. A wounded reminder, yes, but a reminder nevertheless. Communal participation in the universe of popular religion is an equally strong reminder of our shared reality and of our solidarity in the same hope. Few components of Hispanic cultures can so express solidarity and community as popular religiosity can.

Popular Religiosity and the Disclosure of Humanness

Earlier I stated that the will of God is the full humanization of the human race and of each individual within it. God's fundamental will for us is that we become the images of God we already are. I also said that dehumanization, the attempt at derailing that foundational will, is equal to sin.

If it is true that popular religiosity is a privileged locus for Hispanic self-disclosure, then it is there (even if not exclusively) that we must seek to learn what humanness means for Hispanics. In that milieu we can discover the battleground between the processes of humanization and dehumanization as they occur historically in Hispanic cultures. And it is there that fundamental Hispanic cultural values, communicated through popular religiosity, can be perceived as vehicles for the experience of grace.

It is simply impossible, within the limits of this chapter, to do a thorough study of Hispanic popular religiosity, aimed at discovering within it every single component of an implied but real operative definition of what it means to be human. The same must be said in reference to each struggle between humanization and dehumanization, and to each authentic cultural value. I have chosen, instead, to limit myself to a presentation of the two dimensions that seem to be at the core of all others.

A close study of Catholic Hispanic popular religiosity will show that the family is of paramount importance.[27] It seems evident that our family structures and functioning (albeit in an idealized or stylized mode) have been projected onto popular religiosity.

The ways Hispanics relate to God are very similar to the father-child relationship. The father is the authority at home, sets the rules, works hard for the family, but usually expresses little tenderness or human warmth. The children respect him and perhaps even have some fear of him, but ultimately they know that the father loves and sincerely cares for them.

The role of the mother is also projected onto popular religiosity's esteem for Mary, the mother of Jesus. A Hispanic mother is the loving center of the family, she is the one who usually shows tenderness and warm affection and who makes sure that the children understand the father and that he understands the children. She is the conciliator, the one who smooths things out for all in the family.

Relatives, neighbors, and friends are also projected onto popular religiosity in the way Hispanics deal with saints. The networks of the extended family, the godparents, the neighborhood, and others, serve as the model for relations with saints. In the Hispanic family-world one must keep in touch with co-members of these networks, remember birthdays and anniversaries, attend weddings, funerals, and other gatherings, be ready to lend a hand when a member might be in need. Likewise, it is expected that all relations and friends will offer support and help when one in turn is in need. Not to fulfill one's network obligations is extremely rude and offensive. However, close

27. The importance of the family for Hispanic culture in general, and within popular religiosity in particular, has been well documented. As examples, see Elizondo, *Christianity and Culture*, 158–64; Abalos, *Latinos in the United States*, 62–80; A. Mirandé, *The Chicano Experience: An Alternative Perspective* (Notre Dame, Ind.: University of Notre Dame Press, 1985), 146–64.

examination of this web of relations, obligations, and expectations will reveal a deep sense of solidarity and implied mutual trust, and not mainly a calculated quid pro quo contract.

Popular religiosity, as locus of Hispanic self-disclosure, points directly to family and community as two extremely important and evident elements of our cultures. Whatever else can be said about a Hispanic understanding of what it means to be human, this necessarily must include the familial and communal dimensions. The individual is valued and important *because* he or she is a member of a family and of a community. Individual rights are respected and individual achievement encouraged, but within the familial and communal networks that sustain and give meaning to all.[28] Anglo-style individualism is foreign to the Hispanic way of being human. Given the continuous pressure of the dominant Anglo culture on the Hispanic universe, it was inevitable that the virus of this individualism would start seeping into our cultural fabric, creating tension and destruction in our family and community structures and functions. It is also inevitable that this Anglo individualism will affect, as a consequence, Hispanic popular religiosity because, as we have just seen, the latter is a religious extension of the family and community.

From this quick examination of popular religiosity we have retrieved family and community as two key dimensions of being "Hispanically" human. Joined to these are the concomitant dimensions of solidarity and mutual trust, since these two seem to be the sustaining, necessary components of the former. One may say, therefore, that the processes of humanization among Hispanics would promote solidarity and mutual trust (the pillars

28. On the Hispanic sense of relation between the individual and community vis-à-vis Anglo individualism, see Roberto S. Goizueta's excellent article "U.S. Hispanic Theology and the Challenge of Pluralism," in *Frontiers*, ed. Deck.

of family and community), while the processes of dehumanization would lead to the weakening of these through insistence
on individualism.

Popular Religiosity and the Solidarity of Grace

As has been repeated in this chapter, the purpose of our
creation is to be images of God, and the God whose image we
are is the God who is love. This means that to be human is to
be an image of God, an image of love. It is not hard to see the
connection between this concept and the solidarity and mutual
trust embedded in Hispanic cultures and disclosed by popular
religiosity. But we must do more than merely point to the fact
that they seem to connect.

As also mentioned earlier, the greatest and definitive bestowal
of God's love for us occurred in the person of Jesus of Nazareth.
It can be claimed that Jesus is grace incarnate, the loving favor
of God-for-us made human flesh. In turn, the definitive do-
nation of Jesus himself happened on the cross.

It seems to me that the frequent devotion to the cross in
Hispanic popular religiosity, as well as the special place that
Good Friday and the iconography of the suffering Christ hold
for us, point to an important link between Jesus' act of self-
giving love and authentically Hispanic experience. For most
Hispanics, suffering and poverty, unfair treatment and discrimination are part of daily life. For most Hispanics the experience
of crucifixion is not a mere religious event remembered during
liturgical services. The cross is part of life. Masochistic acceptance of suffering, however, is not part of the Hispanic experience. The struggles of daily life and the rich symbols and rituals
of popular religiosity constantly point to an explicit or implied
rejection of this suffering. Few give up, and fewer still pray for
more misery.

When the cross is experienced, Hispanics do not call on a
God of brutal might. The crucified Jesus, weak and suffering

as they are weak and suffering, is the one they turn to. There is solidarity in suffering here. Christ and the people relate at the cross because it is their shared experience. Both Jesus and the people hope for resurrection, but this hope does not take the pain away. It gives it meaning, and it keeps the struggle for the future alive. In other words, if the death of Jesus on the cross is the definitive bestowal of God's love for us, the definitive gift of grace, then Hispanics experience the grace of God and the God of grace, at fundamental moments of their existence, when they turn to the crucified Christ whom they experience in solidarity. They do so, however, through the culturally authentic and communal symbols of popular religiosity.

The cross, as Christians believe, is not the last word. There is the resurrection. For most Hispanics, still crucified by poverty and discrimination, resurrection is only a hope. I am not implying that as Christians we do not believe in the risen Christ. Of course we do! But our daily experience is not yet "risen." Life and popular religiosity are quick to remind us. But if solidarity unites us to Jesus on the cross, mutual trust can make us hope that he will not forget us. In other words, the familial and communal dimensions, as projected onto popular religiosity, can make us hope and continue the struggle. The symbols and rites of popular religiosity, in their process of being molded and remolded, are already showing new signs of this hope.

However, one must candidly admit that resurrection is not as strongly symbolized and expressed in popular religiosity as solidarity in suffering is. The love of a God who can share our wounded condition is certainly present, and this is extremely important. But, as I said earlier, popular religiosity is itself wounded, and it stands in need of saving grace as much as any other human creation. It conveys only one—though crucial—dimension of the gift of God. The other is the possibility of actual new life beyond the symbolic; a new life of real historical justice and reconciliation with God and with neighbor.

Humanization Through Liberation: The Aim of Grace

We are created and called to be images of the God who is love, and here we find the truest definition of what it means to be human. Grace, which is God-for-and-within-us, invites and helps us to move in that direction. That is what humanization is all about.

As Christians, we believe in the Trinity. This necessarily implies that we are also created to image community. To put it another way, the need to love God and the need to love neighbor are intimately linked at the depth of our being human because oneness and community are unconditionally linked in God. It is as impossible to be truly human without reference to God as it is without reference to neighbor. Humanization, the grace-moved process through which we grow into full humanness, must not only lead to the proper relationship with God (which theology has traditionally called by terms such as *justification*), but it must also lead to the proper relationship with neighbor (which we may refer to by such terms as *justice, reconciliation,* or *liberation*).[29] Just as the most correct attitude toward God is unconditional love, so it must also be toward neighbor. Furthermore, ever since Jesus' radical preaching and life, there is no other means given us to love God but the love of neighbor.

Most Christians know what it means to love and serve our neighbor when we speak of specific, individual needs. Someone in need of food, of shelter, of a shoulder to cry on, and so on, will find many Christians ready to provide whatever might be needed. This willingness to serve, of course, is necessary and good.

Most Christians, remembering the well-known story of the person who beyond needing the fish had to be taught how to fish, will also help create institutions and programs to give the

29. Compare de França Miranda, *Libertados para a práxis da justiça*, 95–107.

needy neighbor the tools and motivations to "make it" in society. This form of service too is necessary and good.

But there is another and greater need, requiring a courage and a love that seem beyond human abilities. How do we love our neighbor, and hence love God, when we find ourselves in a society and a world that are built on greed, on injustice, on oppression, on stark individualism, on the quest for success at the expense of the neighbor? We might fall into the temptation of feeling that if we do individual charity, the world will somehow fix itself. We might also fall into the trap of thinking that we only have to look for the ideal trick (such as educational progress and scientific research), and all things will ultimately work themselves out for the good. Or, at the worst, we might conclude that the price of future progress for all is the present suffering and deprivation of most.

I am not implying that we should not do individual charity or that we should do no research and educate no one. As an educator I am certainly not proposing that. What I am questioning is the attitude that views human effort alone—whatever that effort might be—as if it were some kind of trick to be played, as the sole or main cause that will effect the profound changes this world needs. Obviously, Christian morality rejects the notion that future progress ever justifies the death, hunger, or oppression of millions today.

How does one truly and effectively love one's neighbor in a world like ours, especially when we remember that to be human we must love? Is it enough to give the proverbial fish? Is it enough to teach how to fish? What happens when the one who just learned how to fish goes to the water God created for all and finds a fence around it? Do we just look the other way and pretend that we have loved enough? Should we not join in taking the barriers down? Should we not make sure that the fences never go up again? Should we not try, above all, to help everyone discover that the barriers dehumanize both those locked out as well as those who built them? Perhaps the most difficult and most necessary way of loving the neighbor (and thus, of responding to God's grace) is the way we have called reconciliation, justice, or liberation.

By these I mean the establishment of the proper relationship between individuals, societies, and cultures, so that, as a direct result, this world can be truly just and fair for all. But just as in the case of the proper relationship with God that we call justification, reconciliation cannot happen without the initiative and sustaining favor of God. Love cannot happen without the One who is love.

Justice and liberation are other names for love, but for a love that moves beyond the individual plane to become effective at the level of the socioeconomic and political structures. Human reconciliation will not occur truthfully until it happens at this level. I will readily grant that there is no easy recipe.

Jesus of Nazareth claimed that, with him, the reign of God was dawning on this earth.[30] A reign truly began with him but would be fully realized only in the future. He gave us no recipes, no detailed road map, no dates as to when the reign would finally come to its fullness. He seems to have explicitly insisted that not even he knew. But what he did give us was the commandment to love our neighbor, radically and selflessly, pointing to this as the best way of loving God. And if we loved the more needy, more oppressed, more rejected or discriminated neighbor, then the more clearly the reign of God and the God of the reign would be made present among us.

How do we love in this complex, greedy, and suffering world we have inherited? Jesus left us no specific instructions, just the

30. See Mark 1:15 and parallels. The literature on the reign of God, as the core of Jesus' message, is vast and well known. Perhaps R. Schnackenburg's *Gottes Herrschaft und Reich* (Freiburg: Herder, 1965) remains a classic on the subject. See also J. I. González Faus, *Clamor del Reino: Estudio sobre los milagros de Jesús* (Salamanca: Sígueme, 1982); and J. L. Segundo, *El hombre de hoy ante Jesús de Nazaret* (Madrid: Ediciones Cristiandad, 1982), II/1, 105–250.

commandment to go and search out the needy, oppressed, and discriminated neighbors of today, and heal them. To heal in our contemporary world must involve the individual's caring actions for another individual. But—back to the example of the fence around the water—healing today must also include concerted actions that effectively heal societies and cultures.

In our Hispanic context, individual actions are certainly needed. And the worldview of popular religiosity does emphasize them. But the new life we desperately need, the resurrection we hope for, the proper relationship with the neighbor, will only happen through the liberation of our people and the reconciliation of all. This in turn will not happen without God. Popular religiosity, though believing that the world need not be as it is, does not seem to express the explicit commitment or the means (not even symbolic) whereby we might move to establish justice and reconciliation at levels beyond the individual.

If I keep insisting, on the one hand, that we need to love at the level of structures in order to achieve justice and reconciliation, and, on the other hand, that we cannot do this without God and God's grace, it is because I do not believe that these are two separate quests. One cannot choose between strict Pelagianism and exaggerated Augustinianism.[31] As I said before, we are created in the image of a God who is one and triune, which implies that God and neighbor are bound together irrevocably at our deepest level of being. The historical concretization of this unity is the process we call humanization, our way of becoming more fully human.

How does God's grace move us along the path of humanization, helping us establish a more proper relationship with God and with neighbor, in such a way that love can more effectively

31. As synthetic references, see: A. Zumkeller, "Escuela agustiniana," in *Sacramentum Mundi*, I, 81–84; and H. Rondet, "Pelagianismo," ibid., V, 379–83.

further the cause of justice and reconciliation? First of all, Catholic tradition has always insisted that without human cooperation we cannot expect to arrive at either relationship. Catholic tradition has also held that whatever good humans do is a consequence of the action of God's grace.[32] This is not the place to argue the point or the reasons for this dual insistence on the part of Catholicism. Suffice it to say that the arguments lie somewhere between strict Pelagianism and exaggerated Augustinianism.

The grace of God moves us along the path of humanization by liberating our freedom—not for the sake of our merely being free, but rather for the sake of love, since freedom is a necessary condition for true love. Grace frees us from the bondage of chosen dehumanization. Although we will always experience the wounds of sin, the choices of our human will need not be dehumanizing. Grace frees us when, encountering and experiencing the God who offers us love without limits, without conditions, and without exceptions, we accept the gift. When we allow ourselves to be loved unconditionally, then we are set on the path of humanization, because implied in this acceptance is the recognition that love—and only love—can make us humanly whole. Our freedom, as a consequence, is liberated to respond through actions that express love as the purpose and definition of our liberated, new, "risen" life. Without public actions of service and of liberating love, it can be doubted that

32. Perhaps one of the most straightforward texts from the tradition is chapter 5 of the Council of Trent's "Decree on Justification" (1547). See Denzinger (ed. 31a.), n.797. Modern Catholic theology, though going beyond Trent, has not contradicted it. For an interesting contribution by Protestant scholars, compare C. H. Pinnock, ed., *The Grace of God and the Will of Man* (Grand Rapids, Mich.: Zondervan, 1989). Useful on this subject is the fine volume that resulted from the sixth theological and officially sponsored dialogue between Lutherans and Roman Catholics: H. G. Anderson, T. A. Murphy, and J. A. Burgess, eds., *Justification by Faith* (Minneapolis: Augsburg Publishing House, 1985).

there has been authentic acceptance of the love of God. Grace, in other words, makes people free with a freedom to love.

What is said of the individual, however, can be said of communities and societies. Grace also makes peoples and societies free. And just as at the individual level the proof of grace's liberating action is the person's new life of freedom and love for others, so it is at the social level. The struggle for justice, as it involves whole communities and aims at transforming society, is clear proof that the grace of God and the God of grace are actively involved in the humanization process, not only of individuals but of whole communities and of society at large. Left to themselves, human individuals and societies would only continue down the path of dehumanization toward ultimate perdition and self-destruction. But when individuals and societies fight for what is honorable and fair, just and good, there we can detect the God of grace acting within human reality. The grace of God is not "churchy," limited to explicitly religious rituals, gatherings, or feelings. The grace of God, since it is God's very self for us, is active in the entirety of human complexity, at every level. We might call this active, public grace by other names, but this difference in terminology would not cancel the foundational reality.

How does grace lead us to establish proper relationships with God and neighbor? By moving the cause of liberation both in individuals and in societies. And the proof is in the actions and decisions that lead us down the path of humanization, which is ultimately the path of love.

A People's Hope

We have seen that the God of Christians is the one and triune God who is love. This love is given first through creation, thus making humans graced by the fact of their existence. We have also seen that, given that we are created as images of God, the truest definition of what it means to be human must be found precisely in our being that which we are—images of the God who is love. To be human is to image God and, thus, to image love, individually and communally.

We have discussed the fundamental God-imprinted calling to become more fully human. We called this process humanization. We have also recalled that, by human choice, there is within and around us another process that leads us away from this foundational call, dehumanization (which we have identified with sin).

We covered culture's place in the process of humanization and, particularly, we looked at the role of Hispanic culture and its relation to grace. We also saw popular religiosity as a privileged locus of Hispanic self-disclosure, and through it discovered the important place that solidarity holds in Hispanic culture and faith. But we also found that popular religiosity, by itself, lacks some key elements needed in a proper understanding of grace. We had to move beyond popular religiosity, then, in order to discover the liberating effects of grace.

I am aware of the fact that many topics covered in this chapter merit further discussion than they can receive here. There is a need for further study and reflection on the theology of grace as it might be experienced in our Hispanic communities. But one point that I hope has been emphasized and made clear is the intimate connection between the grace of God and our humanness; more specifically, that the grace of God calls and moves us to further our humanization. This will only happen as we open ourselves to the liberating, gracious, and unconditional love of our God, on the one hand, and to the struggle for justice in our society, on the other. The proof of grace is not in religious experience but in the love of neighbor—a love that works justice.

It is evident, it seems to me, that the majority of U.S. Hispanics suffer conditions of poverty and discrimination that directly contradict the will of God. These conditions work against our people's process of humanization. To accept God's liberating love requires our commitment to that humanization and, in the Hispanic context, this means commitment to liberation and justice at the individual and social levels. Popular religiosity tells us of our people's hope. It tells us of the importance of solidarity, and it tells us that our people do experience God as being in solidarity with them. However, this bond of the crucified of today with the cross of Jesus is called by grace to move beyond hope to an active, effective love that works for justice and reconciliation.